Marriage and the Public Good: Ten Principles

Second Edition

Published by the Witherspoon Institute
Princeton, New Jersey
October 2022

Published in the United States by the Witherspoon Institute.
16 Stockton Street, Princeton, New Jersey 08540

Library of Congress Control Number: 2022918298

ISBN: 9798218083427

Printed in the United States of America

www.winst.org

Contents

This book is the second edition of *Marriage and the Public Good: Ten Principles*, the outcome of scholarly research directed by the Witherspoon Institute in Princeton, New Jersey. It brings together scholarship from economics, history, law, philosophy, psychiatry, and sociology to show why marriage—understood in the traditional manner (that is, the durable, loving union of one husband and one wife)—holds tremendous value for the public interest.

W

Executive Summary

We define marriage as a legally sanctioned union of one man and one woman who pledge perpetual fidelity and care to one another. Its existence plays a vital role in preserving the common good and promoting the welfare of children. In virtually every known human society, the institution of marriage provides order and meaning to adult sexual relationships and, more fundamentally, furnishes the ideal context for the bearing and rearing of the young. The health of marriage is particularly important in a free society such as our own, which depends upon citizens to govern their private lives and rear their children responsibly, so as to moderate the scope, size, and power of the state. Marriage is also an important source of social, human, and financial capital for children, especially for those growing up in poor, disadvantaged communities with limited access to such resources. Thus, from the point of view of spouses, children, society, and the polity, marriage as traditionally understood advances the public interest.

Marriage as an institution has been weakening in the United States for decades, with serious negative consequences for society as a whole. Four developments continue to be especially troubling: increases in rates of *divorce*, of *nonmarital childbearing*, and of the notoriously fragile union of *cohabitation*, as well as the normalization of *same-sex marriage*, now civilly lawful in the United States.

We remain persuaded that the case for marriage should be made for the sake of all Americans, and that it *can* be made by reason alone, apart from

1

religious considerations or overly sentimental conservatism. We also believe it is more important than ever to do so effectively and persistently—to avoid further tragic outcomes for our citizens and the breakdown of some invaluable social resources.

Evidence from scientific research confirms that marriage serves women, men, children, and the common good. It offers spouses a benefit they can acquire in no other way: a mutual and complete partnership, a total giving of the self. The health of these partnerships is particularly important in a free society, which depends upon citizens to govern their private lives and rear their children responsibly, so as to limit the scope, size, and power of the state. Other benefits to married adults include *greater financial, emotional,* and *physical well-being,* as well as a *more wholesome society* overall. The nation's retreat from marriage in both practice and in law has been particularly consequential for our most vulnerable communities: children, minorities, and the poor, who pay a disproportionately heavy price for divorce and nonmarital childbearing. In recent years, the working class has been increasingly negatively impacted as well. Children of married parents, however, enjoy the strong start in life provided by *shared biology* with their caregivers, parents' sex-linked *complementarity,* and added *stability* during life's tender years. Thus, marriage understood as the enduring union of husband and wife is both a good in itself and also an advancement of the public interest.

We affirm the following ten principles that summarize the value of marriage:

1. Marriage is a personal union of husband and wife, intended for mutual care throughout the whole of life.

2. Marriage is a profound human good, elevating and perfecting our social and sexual nature.

3. Ordinarily, both men and women who marry are better off as a result.

4. Marriage protects and promotes the well-being of children.

5. Marriage sustains civil society and promotes the common good.

6. Marriage is a wealth-creating institution, increasing human and social capital.

7. When marriage weakens, the equality gap widens.

8. A functional marriage culture fosters political liberty and reduces the burden on government programs.

9. Laws governing marriage matter significantly.

10. "Civil marriage" and "religious marriage" ought not be isolated from one another.

These understandings about marriage are the cross-cultural fruit of broad human experience, reflection, and considerable social-scientific evidence. But a marriage culture cannot flourish in a society whose primary institutions—universities, courts, legislatures, and many religious congregations—not only fail to defend marriage but actively work to subvert it. Their efforts have culminated in the legal alteration of the very structure of marriage, subverting the meaning of the marital union.

Creating a vital marriage culture is not a job for the government. Families, religious communities, and civic institutions must point the way. But law and public policy are also teachers; they will either reinforce and support these goals or undermine them. We call upon our nation's leaders, and our fellow citizens, to support laws and public policies that renew and strengthen our damaged marriage culture through the following actions:

1. Maintain the legal distinction between married and cohabiting couples.

2. Investigate divorce-law reforms.

3. End marriage penalties for low-income Americans.

4.   Protect and expand prochild and profamily provisions in our tax code.

5.   Protect the interests of children against a powerful fertility industry.

6.   Protect the freedom to live out and express belief in the uniqueness of traditional marriage without fear of government coercion and institutional hostility.

7.   Protect the freedom to conduct scholarly inquiry and promote dissemination of accurate research findings on marriage and related topics.

8.   Restore the understanding of marriage as uniquely the union of one man and one woman in lifelong caretaking exclusivity.

Families, religious communities, community organizations, and public policymakers must work together toward a great goal: renewing and strengthening our culture's understanding and practice of marriage so that each year more children are raised by their own mother and father in loving, lasting marital unions. The future of the American experiment depends upon it, and our children deserve nothing less.

W

I

Marriage and the Public Good:
Ten Principles

1 **Marriage is a personal union of husband and wife, intended for mutual care throughout the whole of life.** As a sexual, emotional, financial, legal, spiritual, and parental union, marriage differs from other valued personal relationships in its purposes and intensity. Marriage as historically understood is not the ratification of an existing relationship; it is the beginning of a profoundly new kind of relationship between a man and a woman. They choose to limit their own freedoms in order to gain wondrous new ones, pledging their sexual fidelity to one another, promising loving mutual care and support, and forming a family that welcomes and nurtures the children that their union may engender. This understanding of marriage has predominated in Europe and America for most of the past two thousand years. It naturally emerges from the biological, psychological, and social complementarity of the male and female sexes. This promise of mutual dependence, appreciation, and obligation, solemnized by a legal oath, is strengthened by the pledge of permanence that husband and wife offer to one another—always to remain, never to abandon, even and especially in the most difficult times.

2. Marriage is a profound human good, elevating and perfecting our social and sexual nature. Human beings are social animals, and the social institution of traditional marriage is a profound human good, fundamentally rooted in the spouses' sexual complementarity and procreative possibilities. It creates clear ties of begetting and belonging—ties of identity, kinship, and mutual interdependence and responsibility. These bonds encourage maturity

7

and generosity, so they serve a crucial public purpose. It is only proper for the state to recognize and encourage traditional marriage in both law and public policy. Indeed, it is not surprising that marriage is publicly sanctioned and promoted in virtually every known society and often solemnized by religious and cultural rituals. Modern biological and social sciences continue to confirm the benefits of marriage as a human good consistent with our given nature as sexual and social beings.

3. Ordinarily, both men and women who marry are better off as a result. Married men gain moral and personal discipline, a stable and supportive domestic life, and the opportunity to participate in the upbringing of their children. Married women gain stability and protection, acknowledgment of the paternity of their children, and shared responsibility and emotional support in the raising of those children. Both spouses profit from a mutual commitment to the marital union—including the benefits that come from faithfully fulfilling one's chosen duties as mother or father, husband or wife. The commitment itself is ameliorative; couples who share a moral commitment to marital permanence and fidelity tend to have better marriages. The union assumes an ethic enjoining respect and care, as well as forbidding violence or abuse.

4. Marriage protects and promotes the well-being of children. The family environment provided by marriage allows children to grow, mature, and flourish. It is a seedbed of sociability and virtue for the young, who learn from both their parents and their siblings. Specifically, the traditional married family satisfies children's need to know their biological origins, connects them to both a mother and a father, establishes a framework of love for nurturing them, oversees their education and personal development, and anchors their identity as they learn to move about the larger world. These are not merely desirable goods, but what we owe to children as vulnerable beings filled with potential. Whenever humanly possible, children have a natural human right to know their biological mother and father, and mothers and fathers have a solemn obligation to love their children unconditionally.

5. Marriage sustains civil society and promotes the common good. Civil society tremendously benefits from a stable marital order. Families are themselves small societies, and the web of trust they establish across generations and between the spouses' original families is a key constituent of society as a whole. The network of relatives and in-laws that marriage creates and sustains composes the kind of social capital that facilitates beneficial civic associations and charitable groups. Virtues acquired within the family—generosity, self-sacrifice, trust, self-discipline—are crucial for success in every domain of social life. Children who grow up in broken families often fail to acquire these elemental habits of character. When marital breakdown or the failure to form marriages becomes widespread, society is harmed by a host of social pathologies, including increased poverty, mental illness, crime, illegal drug use, clinical depression, and suicide.

6. Marriage is a wealth-creating institution, increasing human and social capital. The modern economy and modern democratic state depend upon these families to produce the next generation of productive workers and taxpayers. This ongoing renewal of human capital is a crucial ingredient that is now in grave peril in those societies with rapidly aging populations and below-replacement fertility rates. It is within stable (and so, statistically, married) families that young people develop stable patterns of work and self-reliance at the direction of their parents, and this training in turn provides the basis for developing useful skills and gaining a profession. In adults, marriage realigns personal interests beyond the good of the present self, and thus reduces the tendency of individuals and groups to make rash or imprudent decisions that squander the inheritance of future generations. Family networks created by marriage have also provided the foundation for countless entrepreneurial, small-business enterprises (some of which are now large corporations), which are crucial to the vitality of the nation's economy. In addition, devoted spouses and grown children assist in caring for their sick and elderly, maintaining the solvency of pension and social-insurance programs by providing unremunerated care for their loved ones. Without flourishing families established by marriage, in other words, the long-term health of the modern economy would be imperiled.

7. When marriage weakens, the equality gap widens. Poorer children disproportionally suffer from the disadvantages of growing up in a home without a committed mother and father. Children whose parents fail to get and stay married are at an increased risk of poverty, dependency, substance abuse, educational failure, juvenile delinquency, early unwed pregnancy, and a host of other destructive behaviors. When whole families and neighborhoods become dominated by fatherless homes, these risks increase even further. The breakdown of marriage has hit the African American community especially hard. It threatens the cherished American ideal of equal opportunity by depriving adults and especially children of the social capital they need in order to flourish. Precisely because we seek to eliminate social disadvantages based upon race and class, we view the cultural, economic, and other barriers to strengthening marriage in poor neighborhoods—especially among those racial minorities with disproportionately high rates of family breakdown—as a serious problem to be solved with persistence, generosity, and ingenuity.

8. A functional marriage culture fosters political liberty and limited government. Strong, intact marriages create families that stabilize the state and decrease the need for costly and intrusive bureaucratic social agencies. Such families provide for their vulnerable members, produce new citizens with virtues such as loyalty and generosity, and engender concern for the common good. When families break down, crime and social disorder soar, and the state must expand to reassert social control—with intrusive policing, a sprawling prison system, child-support enforcement, and court-directed family life.[1] Without stable families, personal liberty is thus imperiled, as the state tries to fulfill through coercion those functions that families, at their best, fulfill through covenantal devotion.

9. Laws governing marriage matter significantly. Law and culture exhibit a dynamic relationship; changes in one ultimately yield changes in the other. Together, law and culture structure the options that individuals see as available, acceptable, and worthy of choosing. One need only look at the divorce rates that followed changes in divorce law to see that the legal loosening of the marital bond in turn loosened it in the hearts and minds of individuals, who were then entering into marriage with an altered understanding.[2] Given the clear social benefits of traditional marriage, the state has an abundance of compelling reasons to specifically endorse, in both procedure and outcome, traditional marriage over various alternative family-structure options, including same-sex marriage. Since the federal mandate endorsing same-sex marriage, the fundamental structure of marriage—rooted in the inherently procreative nature of an opposite-sex, exclusive union—is witnessing a public transformation. The legal advance and implications have been swift. Demands have increased to redefine civil marriage as a private contract among two, three, or any number of individuals, with any number of abnormal allowances. Others have advocated that the concept of marriage should descend from its aspiration to permanence toward a temporality and/or solubility. Thus through the apparatus of the law, the state has effectively undermined any and all of the social norms which encouraged marriage as historically understood.[3] As the social costs of marital and family breakdown are perceptibly and increasingly grave, and the public goods uniquely provided by marriage recognizable by reasonable persons (regardless of religious or secular worldview), we appeal to the state to search out ways to renew and strengthen traditional marriage norms in law and public policy.

It is also critically important to protect by law the conscience rights and religious liberty of individuals and groups whose convictions hold that marriage has a divine origin that renders it humanly unalterable. These Americans must be defended against erroneous charges of bigotry and protected from demands that they subordinate their religious practice to current cultural movements. As much as popular figures may seek to dictate which moral teachings deserve discarding,[4] our country continues to affirm the free exercise of religion, and for the majority of religious individuals, the meaning of marriage is inextricably bound to their beliefs.

10. "Civil marriage" and "religious marriage" ought not be isolated from one another. Americans have always recognized the right of any person, religious or otherwise, to marry. While the ceremonial forms of religious and secular marriages often differ, the meaning of such marriages within the social order has always been similar. Current social-science evidence on religion and marital success affirms the wisdom of this American tradition, which also acknowledges the positive role that religion plays in creating and sustaining marriage as a social institution.[5] While the ceremonial forms of religious and secular marriages often differ, the meaning of such marriages within the social order has always been similar, to make a pledge before the highest

institutional authority the couple recognizes, be it the state or God, so as to solemnize the promise to the greatest extent possible. It is thus important to recognize the crucial role played by religious institutions in a sustainable marriage culture. Civil marriage and religious marriage are natural allies. It is in the state's interest to promote stability, and stable marriages are even more likely to be forged in the context of a religious covenant. Legalized same-sex marriage has led not only to a weakening, but a parlous rupture in this shared understanding and natural partnership. It is now more crucial than ever for us to recover the historically shared meaning of marriage as distinct from other arrangements.

W

II

Evidence from the Sciences

Over the past fifty years, American society has experimented with new family forms, such as single parenting, step-parenting, and cohabiting parenting. While no single study is definitive, and there is room for debate over particular consequences, the clear preponderance of the evidence shows that intact, married families provide a host of benefits and protections for adults and are the best possible environment for children, compared to alternative family arrangements. A great deal of research now exists from the anthropological, sociological, psychological, and economic sciences demonstrating strong support for the empirical benefits of marriage.

In the last ten years, however, much research has been specifically aimed at countering and undermining this very evidence. We support rigorous inquiry and well-designed research on all family forms, and we welcome and benefit from intellectual challenges that sharpen our search for scientific truth. However, conceptual attacks against traditional marriage have now extended to an intentional obfuscation of the research field, ranging from suspect research designs to misrepresented or overstated findings that seem to discount the benefits of marriage (while findings in its favor are spuriously discredited or at times even suppressed). Much like with the Supreme Court's same-sex marriage decision, ideological commitments now compete with reason and established evidence. The conflict has begun to threaten aspects of free academic inquiry and the analytic conduct of social science itself.

Despite these threats, the fact remains that in virtually every known human society, the institution of marriage has served and continues to serve three important public purposes, which we will examine more closely in the following sections. First, marriage is the institution through which societies seek to organize the bearing and rearing of children; it is particularly important in ensuring that children have the love and support of their father. Second, marriage provides direction, order, and stability to adult sexual unions and to their economic, social, and biological consequences. Third, marriage civilizes men, furnishing them social status, a sense of purpose, and guiding norms that orient their lives away from vice and toward virtue.[6] Marriage achieves its myriad purposes through both social and biological means. And the scientific evidence, if examined thoroughly and critically, continues to reveal that the unique benefits provided by traditional marriage are not replicated by various alternatives. When marriage is strong, children and adults both tend to flourish; when marriage breaks down, every element of society suffers.

The Well-being of Children

The evidence linking the health of marriage to the welfare of children is definitive; a large body of social-scientific research has emerged in the past four decades indicating that children do best when reared by their mothers and fathers in a married, intact family. A 2002 study by the nonpartisan research institute Child Trends examined the effect of family structure on child well-being. Conducted specifically to better inform public policy, the study summarized scholarly consensus on marriage this way: "Research clearly demonstrates that family structure matters for children, and the family structure that helps children the most is a family headed by two biological parents in a low-conflict marriage."[7] Other reviews of the literature on marriage and the well-being of children, conducted by the Brookings Institution, the Princeton School of Public and International Affairs (formerly the Woodrow Wilson School of Public and International Affairs) at Princeton University, the Center for Law and Social Policy, and the Institute for American Values, all came to similar conclusions.[8] The undeniable consensus is that family structure affects children in myriad ways. The intact married family model has three distinct advantages over all others: shared biology, sexual complementarity, and stability.[9]

Shared biology. Children raised by their own biological mother and father share an undeniably significant natural bond of kinship. Consider the research on adopted children, which clearly demonstrates that there are, on average, challenges for children when they are deprived of that original biological connection. An extensive 2008 study on adolescents found that adopted children were almost twice as likely to have had contact with a mental health provider than were nonadopted children, and their likelihood of having a disruptive behavioral disorder was also similarly increased. Most strikingly, these risks were present even though the children studied had been adopted as infants.[10]

More recently, studies have shown that being adopted is associated with significantly higher risks of both emotional and health problems as well as behavioral and academic difficulties in school, despite the fact that adoptive parents in general have income and education levels that are well above average.[11] Other studies of adopted children have documented a nearly four-fold greater risk for attempting suicide.[12] One clinic recently documented a statistical overrepresentation of adopted children presenting for gender dysphoria.[13] Put succinctly by journalist Kathleen Kingsbury in her article title, "Adoptees more likely to be troubled."[14]

These study results do not reflect on the quality of adoptive parents at all, and they in no way are meant to disparage adoptive families. On average, such parents are a selective group: they tend to be highly committed and deeply devoted, and they provide loving and stable homes. However, we speak here not of what is good, but of what is best. Honest reflection reminds us that adoption is a concession to the ideal. Evidence reveals that it is in the best interest of children to be raised by their own biological parents whenever possible. Adoption serves as a vital and fulfilling means of repair when that connection is rent.

The two-biological-parent advantage of traditional marriage is also relevant when considering children conceived by artificial reproductive technologies (ART). Research by Yale psychiatrist Kyle Pruett suggests that donor-conceived children reared without fathers have an unmet "hunger for an abiding paternal presence." His research parallels findings from the literature on divorce and single-parenthood.[15]

One 2010 study, the first of its kind, compared the self-reported experiences of adults who were donor conceived, those who had been adopted, and those raised by their biological parents. Donor offspring shared increased risks for negative outcomes similar to those found among adoptees. Both groups were significantly more likely to struggle with serious, negative outcomes such as depression, substance abuse, and delinquency, even when controlling for socioeconomic and other factors. The donor offspring were *more* likely to have faced substance abuse than were the children of adoption.[16] They also struggled more with feelings of confusion and isolation related to their identity than did the adoptees, which confirms child psychiatrist Kyle Pruett's earlier work suggesting that children conceived by ART without known fathers have deep and disturbing questions about their biological and familial origins.[17]

While these complex matters require much more in-depth and long-term study, the plausibility of nonbiological parenting having "no effect" on children is increasingly questionable, especially as more donor-conceived children are now growing into adults and speaking out.[18] In the words of Wendy Kramer, mother of a donor-conceived son and cofounder of a donor-sibling registry, "Many parents use donor conception instead of adoption because a genetic connection is important to them, but then negate the importance of that very same genetic connection when it involves their child's relationship to the 'donor,' the other half of their child's genetic family, ancestry, and medical history."[19] By contrast, children who are reared by their married biological parents are more likely to have a secure sense of their own biological origins and familial identity.

In his award-winning book, *Do Fathers Matter? What Science Is Telling Us about the Parent We've Overlooked*, Paul Raeburn surveys an abundance of scientific research demonstrating that the contributions of biological fathers are far more important than we have previously imagined.[20] From the very beginnings of a child's life, the father's presence/involvement—or absence/disinterest—affects that child profoundly. One study showed that children whose fathers were involved in their mother's pregnancy were nearly four times more likely than those with uninvolved fathers to survive their first year of life. The uninvolved fathers' babies who survived suffered more complications such as premature and underweight births.[21] A study in Georgia found that infants who had no father listed on the birth certificate were twice as likely to die in infancy as those who did, even after adjusting for economic influences.[22]

Research also suggests that the physical presence of a biological father is especially important for the sexual health of girls. First, numerous studies have noted a correlation between father absence and girls experiencing an earlier onset of puberty, in terms of menarche, compared with girls living with their biological fathers. While there are a number of competing hypotheses as to why this might be so (and not all studies have yielded these results), a 2014 quantitative meta-analysis of the research demonstrates a significant correlation.[23] Correlation has also been reported between age at menarche and age at first consensual sexual intercourse.[24] A 2017 study finds that girls who experience family disruption and decreased father presence are more likely to engage in risky sexual behavior than are girls who receive high-quality fathering, even controlling for both genetics and environment.[25] A 2018 study finds clear father-absence effects in terms of increased numbers of casual sexual relationships not only on daughters' sexual histories but on sons' as well.[26]

Girls reared in single-parent or stepfamilies are much more likely to experience a teenage pregnancy and to have a child outside of wedlock than are girls who are reared in an intact, married family.[27] One study found that only 5 percent of girls who grew up in an intact family became pregnant as teenagers, compared to 10 percent of girls whose biological fathers left after they turned six, and 35 percent of girls whose fathers left when they were younger.[28] These results are in keeping with research that has long shown that biological-father absence has to have an effect on girls' sexual and reproductive trajectories.

Research also suggests that girls are significantly more likely to be sexually abused if they are living outside of an intact, married home—in large part because these girls have more contact with unrelated males (such as stepfathers, stepbrothers, and mother's boyfriends).[29] The most recent National

Incidence Study of Child Abuse and Neglect indicates that those children whose single parent had a live-in partner experienced more than eight times the rate of overall maltreatment, over ten times the rate of abuse, and nearly ten times the rate of neglect, compared to children living with married biological parents.[30]

Again, as with adoptive parents, we do applaud the courageous and honorable effort to form healthy alternative families in the absence of the ideal. In general, however, science reveals this to be a great challenge. Studies suggest that biological parents invest more money and time in their offspring than do stepparents.[31] Others have found that stepparent families are less cooperative than intact biological families; thus, a blended family configuration likely reduces the well-being of all children in the household.[32] Even when children live with their own married biological parents, they tend to experience a deleterious effect if a half-sibling is present in the home.[33] In general, evidence highlights how remarriage and the introduction of a stepparent typically do not benefit children as much as anticipated.[34]

A valid critique of some studies showing father-absence effects is that they do not sufficiently account for covariant factors that might be the actual causes of the negative outcomes. One group of investigators, then, isolated forty-seven of the most rigorous, responsible studies and reviewed their findings. They concluded that these higher-quality studies "continue to document negative effects of father absence on child well-being, though these effects are stronger during certain stages of the life course and for certain outcomes." Robust evidence was noted for negative effects of father absence enduring throughout life, such as increased childhood externalizing behavior (such as biting, fighting, disrupting the classroom), elevated adolescent engagement in risky behavior, lower high-school graduation rates, and poorer mental health in adulthood.[35]

This brings us back around to marriage, which is so valuable partly because it helps to bind a child's biological parents to the child over the course of his life, and so avoid these father-absence effects. And because the father's role in family life is more discretionary in our society (and every known human society) than is the mother's role, marriage is particularly important in binding fathers to their children. It positions a man to receive the regular support, direction, and advice of the mother of his children, and it encourages him to pay attention to that input.[36] Cohabiting biological fathers are—on average—less practically and emotionally invested in their children than are those who are married.[37] Unmarried, nonresidential fathers see their children much less often than do married, residential fathers, and what involvement they have is not consistently related to positive outcomes for their children.[38] Even if they see their children regularly, nonresidential fathers are not as able to participate in supervision, oversight, and rule-setting; thus, their "parental" role is not substantive.[39] By contrast, married fathers can exercise an abiding, important, and positive influence on their children, and they are especially likely to do so in a happy marriage.[40] Paul Raeburn's book on fathers concludes, "We often say doing what's best for our kids is more important than anything else we do. What's best for our kids should always include a role for fathers."[41] And as the data demonstrate, marriage is the most reliable way to ensure this "best for our kids" outcome.

Complementarity of the sexes. Studies suggest that men and women bring different strengths to the parenting enterprise.[42] Although there is a good deal of overlap in the talents that mothers and fathers exercise in parenting, there *are* crucial differences. Mothers are more sensitive to the cries, words, and gestures of infants, toddlers, and adolescents, and, partly as a consequence, they are better at physically and emotionally nurturing their children.[43] These special capacities of mothers seem to have deep biological underpinnings: during pregnancy and breast-feeding, women experience high levels of the hormone peptide oxytocin, which fosters affiliative (bonding) behaviors.[44]

Fathers excel when it comes to providing discipline, ensuring safety, and challenging their children to embrace life's opportunities and confront life's difficulties. The greater physical size and strength of most fathers, along with the pitch and inflection of their voice and the directive character of their speaking, give them an advantage when it comes to child training, an advantage that is particularly evident with boys, who are more likely to comply with their father's than their mother's commands.[45] They also engage in physical forms of play with their children that are different from a typical mother's play.[46] Fathers are more likely than mothers to encourage their children to tackle difficult tasks, endure hardship without yielding, and seek out novel experiences.[47]

These paternal strengths also have deep biological underpinnings: fathers typically have higher levels of testosterone—a hormone associated with dominance and assertiveness—than do mothers.[48] One study finds that fathers affect their children's language development by making a "unique contribution" that is both substantial and independent of the contribution of mothers.[49] Mothers and fathers shape their children in distinct ways, and children in turn respond to them distinctly. One study found evidence for this via brain imaging: adult children viewing their parents' faces displayed responses in different areas of the brain when seeing their father's versus their mother's face.[50] Although the link between nature, nurture, and sex-specific parenting talents is undoubtedly complex, one cannot ignore the evidence of sex differences in parenting—differences that marriage builds on to the advantage of children.

Boys benefit from their parents' marriage in unique ways. Research consistently finds that boys raised by their own father and mother in an intact, married family are less likely to experience problems with aggression, attention deficit disorder, delinquency, and school suspensions, compared to boys raised in other family arrangements.[51] Some studies suggest that the negative behavioral consequences of marital breakdown are more significant for boys than for girls. One researcher, investigating father-infant interactions to assess their effects on the child's future behavior, found that the tendency toward bad behavior later was greater when the father's interactions in infancy had been less close and affectionate. These effects were independent of the mother's behavior with the infant and were greater for male infants than for females. Due to childhood externalizing behavior being associated with increased oppositional behavior in adulthood, these effects can have long-range negative impacts.[52] Another study found that boys reared within single-parent and stepfamilies were more than twice as likely to end up in prison, compared to boys reared in an intact family.[53] One study found that men who had fond memories of their fathers from childhood were more stable and better equipped to deal with stress as adults.[54] Clearly, stable marriage and paternal role models are crucial for keeping boys (and the men they become) from self-destructive and socially destructive behavior.

Stability. Trustworthy studies (the only kind we cite), controlling for socioeconomic, demographic, and even genetic factors, have found a solid relationship between instability in family structure and poor child well-being. Hence, the link between family breakdown and youth crime, for instance, is not just an artifact of poverty; it's present no matter the family income.[55] Divorce studies have followed adult twins (one divorced, one not) and their children to distinguish the unique effects of divorce on children, apart from the potential role that genetic and socioeconomic factors might play. What's been plainly revealed is that divorce has negative consequences for children's psychological and social welfare, even after controlling for the genetic vulnerabilities of the parents who divorced.[56] Children trapped in a physically or psychologically injurious situation might be better off with separated or legally divorced parents. Thankfully, however, these cases are the extreme minority. The intact married home continues to provide, on average, unparalleled stability for children, and these children are less apt to experience adverse transitions that disrupt their development and continuity of care.

The stability of the intact married home also significantly affects educational outcomes. Preschool children reared there are substantially more likely to be involved in literacy activities (such as being read to by adults or learning to recognize letters), and they score higher in reading comprehension later as fourth graders.[57] Kindergartners from cohabiting households tend to have lower reading scores than do their same-age peers. Interestingly, these differences persist when controlling for other factors and manifest whether they are living with both biological parents *or* one parent and a partner.[58] School-age children from married homes are approximately 30 percent less likely to cut class, be tardy, or miss school altogether, when compared to children in non-intact family situations.[59] Children in intact married households are about twice as likely to graduate from high school, compared to those reared in single-parent or stepfamilies. In one study, 37 percent of children born outside of marriage and 31 percent of children whose parents divorced went on to drop out of high school, compared to 13 percent of children from intact married families.[60] One large, nationwide study of adolescents finds that those from cohabiting households have a 60 percent lower graduation rate than do their peers from intact married homes, even after controlling for variations in income and parent education levels.[61] Children from divorced homes are 44 percent less likely to obtain a bachelor's degree and 29 percent less likely to obtain a graduate degree, even after taking into account the lowered resources available to them.[62]

Consistent with these educational disparities are recent studies on wealth differences between these two groups. Adult children from continuously married homes earn more, work more hours, and are more likely to be married themselves than those from divorced homes.[63] Another study calculated a midlife "wealth penalty," estimated to be at least $61,600, for those who had experienced family breakdown during their childhoods.[64]

The family stability undergirded by marriage fosters not only positive education and career outcomes for that family's children but also their emotional health. Children from stable, married families are significantly less likely to suffer from depression, anxiety, alcohol and drug abuse, and thoughts of suicide, compared to children from divorced homes.[65] One study of the entire population of Swedish children found that Swedish boys and girls in two-parent homes are about 50 percent less likely to suffer from suicide attempts, alcohol and drug abuse, and serious psychiatric illnesses, compared to children reared in single-parent homes.[66] A survey of the American literature on child well-being finds that family structure is more consequential than poverty in predicting children's psychological and behavioral outcomes.[67] In general, children who are reared by their own consistently married mother and father benefit greatly from the resultant stability; they are much more likely to confront the world with a sense of hope, self-confidence, and self-control than are those who experience the trauma of family breakdown during these formative years at home.

Both social and biological mechanisms seem to account for the value of an intact marriage in children's lives. From a sociological perspective, marriage allows families to benefit from shared labor within the household, income streams from two parents, and the economic resources of two sets of kin.[68] A married mom and dad typically invest more time, affection, and oversight into parenting than does a single parent. As importantly, they tend to monitor and improve the parenting of one another, augmenting one another's strengths, balancing one another's weaknesses, and reducing the risk that a child will be abused or neglected by an exhausted or angry parent.[69] The trust and commitment associated with marriage also give the husband and wife a sense that they have a future together, as well as a future with their children. This horizon of commitment, in turn, motivates them to invest practically, emotionally, and financially in their children at higher levels than do cohabiting or single parents.[70]

Over the past several decades, Americans have experimented with various alternatives to marriage, and the evidence is clear: children raised in intact married families generally do better in every area of life than those raised in other family structures. To declare this traditional household as the "gold standard" is not meant to disparage the parents and children in other scenarios. However, as expressed by journalist Alysse ElHage, herself an adult child of divorce, "Just because families come in a variety of forms doesn't mean we should stop striving to repair and rebuild the one family form we know is best for as many children as possible."[71] Those who care about the well-being of children—as every citizen should—ought to care about the health of modern marriage.

The Well-being of Adults

While the most important benefits of marriage redound to children, marriage also holds significant advantages for those who enter into it. Marriage as we've described it benefits people financially, emotionally, physically, and socially. The two sexes do often experience marriage's positive effects in different ways, and for wives, the benefits are more sensitive to the *quality* of the marriage than for husbands.

Financial benefits. The financial advantages of marriage are easy to see. Typically, marriage allows couples to pool resources and share labor within the household. The commitment associated with marriage also provides couples with a long-term outlook that allows them to invest together in housing and other appreciable assets.[72] Similarly, the norms of adult maturity associated with marriage encourage spouses to spend and save in a more responsible fashion.[73] Married men and women are more likely to accumulate wealth and to own a home than are unmarried adults, even similarly situated cohabiting or single adults.[74] Married men earn between 10 and 40 percent more money than do single men with similar professional and educational backgrounds.[75] Men of prime working age who are married also have consistently higher rates of labor-force participation, even when controlling for other factors, such as race and education.[76] Married women generally do not experience a marriage premium in their income, since many women combine marriage with motherhood (which tends to lessen a women's earnings).[77]

The positive effects of marriage on earnings extend across the population spectrum, benefiting minorities similarly to whites. Around 70 percent of married black men are considered middle-class, compared to 44 percent of divorced black men and only 20 percent of those who never married,[78] and married black men experience a marriage premium of at least $12,500 in individual income over their black single peers.[79] In general, even people with little education (regardless of race) enjoy these monetary advantages of marriage.[80] In fact, women from disadvantaged backgrounds are much less likely to fall into poverty if they get and stay married.[81]

Finally, the nation's economy at large can benefit from a strong marriage culture. A recent cross-national study of the relationship between family structure and economic growth found a significant association between the two. Controlling for other factors, a 13 percent increase in marriage rates corresponded with an 8 percent increase in per capita GDP, and every 13 percent increase in the proportion of children living with two-parent families was similarly associated with a 16 percent increase in GDP. In addition, the presence of more two-parent families was linked with less crime and increased personal savings, as well as having a positive association with men's participation in the labor force.[82] The multiple connections between family structure and economic growth are strong and show that "what happens in the family may not affect only the welfare of private families but also the wealth of nations."[83]

Emotional and physical benefits. Marriage also promotes health of the body and mind. A 2016 comprehensive review of the research by Cardus, an independent Canadian think tank, found that "an overwhelmingly large majority of the studies indicates that married couples are happier, healthier, and live longer than those who are not married."[84] The evidence for a "marriage advantage" exists across an impressive array of objective outcomes, including a greater chance of successful cancer recovery, increased cardiovascular health, faster illness recovery, healthier habits and lifestyles, and better responses to psychological distress.[85] One 2013 study found that for five types of cancer, "the survival benefit associated with marriage was larger than the published survival benefit of chemotherapy."[86] Another study found that cardiac surgery patients who were married rather than unmarried were 70 percent less likely to die in the following five years.[87] In terms of general longevity, a meta-analysis conducted on ninety-five studies found a 30 percent greater risk of early death for non-elderly, never-married singles versus married people.[88] As for the elderly, a meta-analysis of fifty-three studies found that the married individuals were 12 percent less likely to have died during the study period.[89] Summarily put by sociologist Michael Rendall and colleagues in 2011, the fact that married adults have lower mortality when compared to the unmarried is a "consistent empirical finding across populations."[90]

Married adults also tend to feel happier and enjoy lower levels of depression and substance abuse than do cohabiting or single adults.[91] Spouses are more likely than nonmarried partners to encourage their counterparts to monitor their health and seek medical help if they are experiencing an illness.[92] The norms of adult maturity and fidelity associated with marriage encourage women and especially men to avoid unhealthy or risky behaviors, from promiscuous sex to heavy alcohol use.[93] The increased wealth and economic stability that come from being married enable men and women to seek better medical care.[94] A "marriage protection effect" against suicide has been documented in numerous studies across decades and social contexts.[95] The emotional support furnished by high-quality, low-conflict marriages reduces stress and thus the stress hormones that often cause ill health and mental illness.[96] An important caveat to note is that low-quality or high-conflict marriages can negatively impact those same physiological systems,[97] as researcher Susan Martinuk points out: "the quality of a marriage is a critical variable in the health benefits that couples enjoy."[98] And interestingly, the one area where marriage tends not to promote a health benefit for couples is weight gain.[99]

However, marriage in general is so powerfully beneficial that health and science writer Kate Lunau boiled it down to this: "If we could package it in a pill, marriage would qualify as a wonder drug."[100]

Societal benefits. Marriage often changes for the better the social lives of both men and women. Of course, not all of these changes can be discussed here, as we must rely on the available scientific evidence for our conclusions. One thing that has been unequivocally shown is that marriage plays a crucial role in civilizing men. It would not be an oversimplification to say that marriage helps make boys into men and men into heroes (at least to their own families). Married men are less likely to commit a crime,[101] to be sexually promiscuous or unfaithful to a longtime partner,[102] or to drink to excess.[103] They also attend church more often, spend more time with kin, and put in more hours at work.[104] A recent study found a "marriage effect" on the sexual behavior choices of married and cohabiting young adults; while both relationship configurations generally expect sexual fidelity, married individuals were significantly less likely than cohabitants to engage in sex outside of their relationship.[105] This finding is consistent with another recent study that found a 30 percent greater likelihood that cohabitants would engage in sex with someone other than their partner (compared to married couples).[106] Longitudinal research by the late University of Virginia sociologist Steven Nock suggests that these effects are not an artifact of selection but rather a direct consequence of marriage. Nock tracked men over time as they transitioned from singlehood to marriage and found that men's behaviors actually changed in the wake of a marriage: After tying the knot, men worked harder, visited bars less often, increased their church attendance, and spent more time with family members.[107] For many men, marriage is a rite of passage that introduces them fully into an adult world of responsibility and self-control. Sadly, our nation's steady retreat from marriage has resulted in vast numbers of men consequently "unburdened and unmoored," contributing to a rise in social problems, according to economists in a 2016 study.[108]

Why *does* marriage play such a crucial role in making men into harder workers, more faithful mates, and more peaceable citizens? Part of the answer is sociological. The norms of trust, fidelity, sacrifice, and providership associated with marriage give men a set of "directions" about how they should act toward their wives and children—norms that are not as clearly applicable to nonmarital relationships.[109] A married man also gains status in the eyes of his wife, her family, their friends, and the larger community when he signals his maturity by marrying.[110] Most men seek to maintain their social status by abiding by society's norms; a society that honors marriage, then, is better poised to produce men who honor their wives and care for their children. Biology also matters for the civilizing of men. Several studies taken together suggest strongly that married men—especially married men with children—are less inclined to experience inflated hormone levels that can contribute to aggressive, promiscuous, and high-risk behavior.[111]

Of course, marriage also matters in unique ways for the social realities of women. A 1994 Justice Department report found that single and divorced women were over four times more likely to be the victim of a violent crime, compared to married women.[112] Married women are also much less likely to be victimized by a partner than are women in a cohabiting or sexually intimate dating relationship.[113] One study found that 13 percent of cohabiting couples had had arguments in the past year that had gotten violent, compared to 4 percent of married couples.[114] Another recent study examined Philadelphia police reports of intimate-partner violence and found that over 80 percent of incidents involved individuals who were not married, with current dating relationships experiencing the highest degrees of violence and injury. Comparatively, only 15 percent of cases involved married couples, while 3.5 percent involved ex-spouses.[115] Some studies suggest that one reason women in nonmarital relationships are more likely to be victimized is that these relationships have higher rates of infidelity, and infidelity invites serious conflict between partners.[116] For most women, therefore, marriage is a safe harbor.

It is not just marital status but the very ideal of marriage that matters. Married persons who value marriage for its own sake—who oppose cohabitation, who think that marriage is for life, and who believe that it is best for children to be reared by a father and a mother as husband and wife—are significantly more likely to experience high-quality marriages, compared to married persons who are less supportive of the union.[117] Men and women committed to the ideal of marriage are also more likely to spend time with one another and to sacrifice for their relationship.[118] This normative commitment is particularly linked for men (more than for women) to spousal devotion.[119] Simply put, men and women who intend to marry for life are more likely to experience a happy marriage than are those who marry with one eye on the exit door.

Vast amounts of research spanning over half a century have provided abundant evidence that marriage improves the lives of those women and men who accept its obligations and believe in its promises. Even so, enormous effort has been put forth of late to counter the established science and undermine solid findings, motivated more by a desire to reshape rather than to accurately inform the cultural understanding of marriage.[120]

Pointing out the empirical benefits of marriage and how it leads to human flourishing neither stigmatizes singles nor denigrates those in other family forms. Some people do not desire marriage and choose the single life, while others would like to be married but never get the opportunity. Others seek same-sex arrangements, or coupled or communal cohabiting situations. All of these persons are endowed with human dignity, and are worthy of respect and kindness. But because marriage between one man and one woman is important for society as a whole and particularly for vulnerable segments of society such as children and the poor, those who choose to embark upon the marital union deserve social encouragement. All citizens deserve an accurate portrayal of marriage to help encourage them toward a potential good, a good which it is in the state's interest to support and protect.

Marriage benefits society as a whole, and some of those benefits redound even to those who choose not to marry. Perhaps some men do not want to be domesticated or do not wish to be burdened with the duties of child rearing, and perhaps some women do not desire what a good marriage uniquely offers, or they choose to prioritize their careers instead. These singles benefit greatly from established, stable families around them who, through friendship, can offer a sense of family, the delight of the presence of children, and a warm respite from the demands of career and the unpredictability of modern coupling. People deserve to know that overall, those who embrace marriage live longer and happier lives than those who do not, and that the freedom found through intentional avoidance of family responsibilities and commitment often later proves unsatisfying.

The Public Consequences of Marital Breakdown

The public consequences of the retreat from marriage are massive and substantial. As the evidence shows, marital breakdown reduces the collective welfare of our children, strains our justice system, weakens civil society, increases the size and scope of governmental power, and contributes to human despair.

Reduced child welfare. Myriad indicators of social well-being demonstrate our point. Take child poverty. One Brookings survey indicates that the increase in child poverty in the United States since the 1970s is due almost entirely to declines in the percentage of children reared in married families, primarily because children in single-parent homes are significantly less likely to receive much material support from their fathers.[121] A 2018 Child Trends report finds that "45 percent of children in the U.S. have experienced at least one adverse childhood experience, with economic hardship and parental divorce or separation the most common nationally and in every state."[122] With these two factors (poverty and divorce) so closely linked, a child facing one often experiences both. Researchers Vanessa Sacks and David Murphey describe adverse childhood experiences as a "critical public health issue"; these events can negatively affect children throughout their lives, manifesting in problems that are also transmissible to the *next* generation: alcoholism, drug abuse, depression, suicide, obesity, etc.[123]

With respect to adolescents, Penn State sociologist Paul Amato estimated how these older children would fare if our society had the same percentage of two-parent biological families as it did in 1960. His research indicates that this nation's adolescents would have 1.2 million fewer school suspensions, one million fewer acts of delinquency or violence, over 746,000 fewer repeated grades, and more than 71,000 fewer suicides.[124] Similar numbers could be estimated for the collective effect of family breakdown on teen pregnancy, depression, and high-school dropout rates. The bottom line is this: Children have paid a heavy price for adult failures to get and stay married, and the most vulnerable communities continue to suffer the greater costs.

Strains on society. Public safety and our justice system have also been affected by the retreat from marriage. Though rates of property and violent crime have in general been falling for years, and the incarceration rate fell to its lowest in twenty years in 2016, the United States still has the largest population of inmates in the world, amounting to almost 2.2 million people. Six and a half million, or one out of every thirty-eight adults in the United States, are under some form of correctional supervision.[125] Public expenditures on criminal justice at the state and local level alone more than tripled from 1977 to 2015, increasing from $58 billion to $181 billion.[126]

Empirical research on family and crime strongly suggests that crime is driven in part by the breakdown of marriage. George Akerlof, a Nobel laureate in economics, argues that the crime increase in the 1970s and 1980s was linked to declines in the marriage rate among young working-class and poor men.[127] Harvard sociologist Robert Sampson concludes from his research on urban crime that murder and robbery rates are closely linked to family structure: "Family structure is one of the strongest, if not the strongest, predictor of variations in urban violence across cities in the United States."[128] One study examined crime at the county level and found an inverse relationship between marriage and crime rates across various types of crime; the higher the marriage rate, the lower the rate of juvenile violence, drug use, and property and violent crime. The results were so striking that researchers concluded that the marriage and crime relationship was even more extensive than previous studies had shown.[129] This close empirical connection between family breakdown and crime suggests that the increased spending on crime fighting, imprisonment, and criminal justice in the United States over the last fifty years is largely the direct or indirect consequence of marital breakdown.

Public spending on social services also has risen dramatically since the 1960s, in large part because of increases in divorce and nonmarital childbearing. Estimates vary regarding the costs to the taxpayer of family breakdown, but they clearly run into the many billions of dollars. One Brookings study found that the retreat from marriage was associated with an increase of $229 billion in welfare expenditures from 1970 to 1996.[130] Another study found that local, state, and federal governments spend $33 billion per year on the direct and indirect costs of divorce—from family-court costs to child-support enforcement to TANF and Medicaid.[131] In 2008, one study estimated that the cost of divorce and nonmarital childbearing to taxpayers was $112 billion in a single year alone.[132]

Increases in divorce also mean that family judges and child-support-enforcement agencies play a deeply intrusive role in the lives of adults and children affected by divorce, setting the terms for such profoundly important arrangements as custody, child visitation, and child support for more than a million adults and children every year. Clearly, when the family fails to govern itself, government steps in to pick up the pieces.

Although there has been no definitive comparative research specifically on state expenditures and family structure (and religion and political culture may also be involved in this relationship), the correlation between the two is suggestive. A retreat from marriage seems to go hand in hand with decreased GDP and more expensive and more intrusive government. We do know that family breakdown leads to growing hardship in disadvantaged communities, making the call for more government intervention—and more government spending—all the more irresistible. It is a pathological spiral, one that only a restoration of marriage can hope to reverse.

Human despair. Anyone affected by suicide knows its devastating effects. As a societal trend, it threatens to inflict untold suffering on our populace. A CDC report revealed that from 1999 to 2016, the overall suicide rate rose nearly 30 percent. Forty-four states had significant increases, and twenty-five of these saw increases *above* 30 percent. While mental-health issues are obvious contributors to the problem, 54 percent of victims in 2015 (from a study of twenty-seven states) had no such known condition.[133]

The wide surge in suicide rates indicates a public health crisis—but a crisis of a particular kind, one affected by a lack of social and interpersonal connectivity. While mental-health care is obviously an important component, behavioral scientist Clay Routledge points out that the surge in suicide is taking place even while treatments for mental conditions have become more effective, available, and utilized. Additional factors are at work, and he proposes that part of the suicide epidemic arises from "a crisis of meaninglessness," pointing to the societal shifts—such as the decline of the family and heightened secularization—which have led to "greater detachment" and a "weaker sense of belonging."[134] These conditions create an elevated risk of "existential despair," which further erodes our sense of belonging and meaningfulness until, perhaps, we can't imagine a life worth living. Routledge cites a study that finds that adults with children are engaged more with "matters of meaning" compared to those without children, and that caring for one's children enriches a person's sense of meaningfulness.[135]

Now consider such commentary in light of the retreat from marriage among the working class. Mortality rates among white, non-Hispanic persons in midlife had been falling for most of the twentieth century but saw a sustained rise from 1998 to 2013. The increase was due primarily to "deaths of despair," which include substance-abuse-induced deaths and suicides. Within this group, extreme disparities existed among education levels: death rates continued to rise for whites with a high-school education or less; they began falling for those with a college degree.[136] Princeton economists Anne Case and (Nobel laureate) Angus Deaton explored the multifaceted forces that could account for this dire reality. They recount that after the early 1970s, the labor-market shift from an industrial to a commercial focus resulted in lower wages for many blue-collar jobs. This situation interacted with changing social ideas about sex and parenting outside of marriage as well as swings away from churches and organized religion. Taken together, these trends were especially impactful for those with lower levels of education; for them, there was "a loss of the structures that give life a meaning."[137] "Lower wages not only brought withdrawal from the labor force, but also made men less marriageable; marriage rates declined, and there was a marked rise in cohabitation."[138] All of this has resulted in a "cumulative disadvantage" for whites with lower education levels, with each successive generation having poorer outcomes than the one that preceded it.[139]

Increasingly, articles and news media celebrate the undoing of marriage as a liberating opportunity for today's adults. As Bella DePaulo recently wrote in

Psychology Today, "Once upon a time, many of the big, important components of adult life came all rolled up in the ball of marriage. Now, the threads have been pulled and are left scattered haphazardly on the ground. Each of us as individuals gets to reassemble them any way we want—or leave them behind and come up with entirely different threads for stitching together just the right life."[140] But while what DePaulo calls "the great unraveling" reads like a fairy tale of freedom to many educated elites, an honest reckoning reveals that much of society, including children, the poor, and increasingly the working class[141] experience it quite differently. They are left holding the scraps of what once was a rich fabric of familial and communal bonds, laboring to piece together a life of meaning with ties that no longer bind.

Four Threats to Marriage

Until fifty years ago, marriage served the vast majority of adults as a nurturing and governing environment for sex, procreation, and child rearing. As we have shown, this protective association has all but unraveled, with serious negative consequences for society as a whole. Four developments from this decoupling of marriage from sex and parenting continue to be especially troubling: divorce, nonmarital births, cohabitation, and same-sex marriage.

Divorce. From 1960 to 2000, increases in divorce doubled the U.S. rate from about 20 percent to about 45 percent of all first marriages.[142] Reviewing data from the years 2006 to 2010, a 2012 National Health Statistics Report concluded that almost a third of all first marriages end in divorce within ten years. By twenty years, 45 percent have ended.[143] There has been, however, a recent reversal; the divorce rate has actually been declining and was 26 percent lower in 2016 than at its zenith in 1980, affecting just over one million women in 2016. (The highest rate in recent years was 1.3 million women in 2008.)[144] The lower divorce rates are seen particularly among young adults, declining 18 percent from 2008 to 2016.[145] It's unclear, though, how good *is* this "good news." The decrease is directly connected with the declining overall *marriage* rate and the increasing *class divide* in American families. Those who marry tend to be better educated and older and therefore (statistically) less likely to divorce, whereas those who are poorer and less educated are increasingly choosing to form relationships and families without marrying at all.[146] One 2017 study found that 56 percent of middle- and upper-class adults are married, compared with only 26 percent of poor and 39 percent of working-class adults.[147] Thus, as put by Bloomberg's Ben Steverman, "Marriage is becoming a more durable, but far more exclusive, institution."[148]

While divorce rates are trending in the right direction, one million divorces per year is still an overwhelming number of family dissolutions. The data suggest that approximately two-thirds of all divorces involving children break up low-conflict marriages, where domestic violence or emotional abuse is not a factor in the divorce.[149] Unfortunately, these children seem to bear the heaviest burden from the divorce of their parents.[150] Children from broken homes are significantly more likely to divorce as adults, experience marital problems, suffer from mental illness and delinquency, drop out of high school, have a poor relationship with one or both parents, and have difficulty committing themselves to a relationship.[151] Furthermore, in most respects, *re*marriage tends to be of little or no help to children of divorce. Those who grow up in stepfamilies experience about the same levels of educational difficulty, teenage pregnancy, and criminal activity as do children who remain in a single-parent family after a divorce.[152] Due to the enduring effects on and lifelong health consequences for children, some researchers have argued that divorce should be treated as a public health crisis.[153]

Divorce is also associated with poverty, depression, substance abuse, and poor health among adults.[154] Additionally, parallel to the points made earlier about marriage's protective effects, divorce is strongly associated with suicide-risk elevation: "That divorced people are at a risk for completed suicide that is greater than that of age matched, married peers is close to a sociological law," noted two scholars in 2015.[155] In examining this risk, one study (more rigorously than others) controlled for potential contributing factors to suicide—such as depression—and also considered the timing of the divorce. Its findings suggest that divorce increases the risk of death by suicide by 60% if recent and 30% if more distant.[156] The benefits of a quality marriage and the negative effects of divorce are so numerous that some research initiatives recommend strengthening and encouraging marriage as one means of lowering societal health-care costs overall.[157] In light of this, the "gray divorce revolution"—the doubling of divorce rates for those over fifty and tripling for those over sixty-five—is very troubling.[158] While rarely involving minor children, these divorces have negative economic, health, and intergenerational family effects that must not be underestimated, as they deleteriously impact the health of society as a whole.[159]

More broadly, widespread divorce undermines the larger marriage culture, insofar as it sows distrust, insecurity, and a low-commitment mentality among married and unmarried adults,[160] thereby contributing to the acceptance of and rise in cohabitation.[161] Couples who take a permissive view of divorce are significantly less likely to invest themselves in their marriages and less likely to be happy in them.[162] For all these reasons, divorce threatens marriage, hurts children, and has had dire consequences for the nation as a whole.

Nonmarital childbearing. The number of children born without the benefit of married parents rose from 5 percent in 1960 to 32 percent in 1995. By 2008, it had increased to 41 percent, and it has remained relatively stable since then.[163] Some of those parents do later marry; most do not. A Pew Research Center analysis of census data found that in 2018, one-third of U.S. children were living with an unmarried parent, up from only 13 percent in 1968.[164] Also in 2018, 30 percent of single-mother households were living in poverty, as were 17 percent of single-father households and 16 percent of cohabiting parents—but only 8 percent of married parents.[165] The rising proportion of nonmarital births is seen across all educational groups[166] and ethnic groups;[167] these births are becoming more normal across all segments of society. But again, the poorer/less educated suffer more. The nonmarital birth rate for white women without a high-school diploma or GED is eight-and-a-half times higher than for those with at least a bachelor's degree (59 percent versus 7 percent).[168] This increasing number of poorer children born either to single mothers or cohabitants are subjected to greater instability, further contributing to the diverging destinies of children from different classes.[169]

The African American community has especially suffered in this area. The marriage rate for black women is significantly lower than for all other racial groups.[170] Only 26 percent of black women were currently married in 2016.[171] In that same year, 70 percent of all births to black mothers occurred outside of marriage.[172] Given that unmarried women experience more unintended pregnancies than do married women, black women (the least likely to be married) disproportionately experience such pregnancies and consequently suffer abortion more than any other minority group.[173] In 2014, their abortion rate was almost three times higher than that of white women.[174] Twenty-eight percent of the nation's abortions,[175] then, were suffered that year by only 13 percent of the population.[176] In New York City, thousands more black babies are aborted every year than are born alive.[177] Those who care about rectifying our nation's class and racial inequalities should care about strengthening the culture of marriage as critical to achieving that goal.

The biggest problem with nonmarital childbearing is that it typically denies children the advantage of having two parents who are committed daily to their emotional and material welfare.[178] As previously discussed, children raised in single-parent families are two to three times more likely to experience serious negative life outcomes such as imprisonment, depression, teenage pregnancy, and high-school incompletion, compared to children from intact, married families[179]—even after controlling for socioeconomic factors (such as income, education level of parents, etc.).

Unsurprisingly, nonmarital childbearing also has negative consequences for the adults involved. Women who bear children outside of marriage are significantly more likely (than their peers who don't) to experience poverty, drop out of high school, and have difficulty finding a good marriage partner.[180] Men who father children outside of marriage are significantly more likely to end up undereducated, to earn less, and to have difficulty finding a good marriage partner.[181] These trends are true even after controlling for socioeconomic factors.

Consider data on the millennial generation. In 2014, 55 percent of millennials (aged twenty-eight through thirty-four that year) had had their first child before marrying. And 72 percent of this group had avoided living in poverty. As a comparison, 95 percent of their peers who married *before* having children were not in poverty. Even among millennials who had grown up in low-income families, 71 percent who married before having children had achieved middle-to-high income status by the time of the study, compared to only 41 percent of those who had had at least one child before marrying.[182]

A growing number of children born outside of marriage are born to cohabiting couples, yet most newborns of unmarried parents will still spend over half of their childhood in a single-parent home. This is in part because the vast majority of cohabiting unions, even ones involving children, end in dissolution.[183] Cumulatively, the rise of nonmarital childbearing has been devastating for children, adults (both men and women), and society.

Cohabitation. Cohabitation rates in the United States rose more than ninefold from 1970 to 2004, increasing from 523,000 couples to five million.[184] Since then, the numbers have continued to skyrocket, increasing to 14 million couples in 2007, and to 18 million in 2016.[185] Cohabitation is now the *typical* first union for young adults.[186]

Despite cohabitation's growing popularity, science shows that cohabitation and marriage are not equivalent choices and do not yield comparable outcomes. Cohabitation does not provide the same degree of protective health effects as marriage,[187] nor do cohabiting couples achieve asset-accumulation levels on par with married couples.[188] The adults in cohabiting unions also suffer higher rates of domestic violence, sexual infidelity, and breakup.[189] These unions are typically more fragile than marriages, perhaps because they do not entail the same level of moral and legal commitment. Cohabitants often do not agree about the status of their relationship, and they typically do not receive as much relationship support from friends and family as married couples do.[190] When cohabitants *do* go on to marry, they are more likely to divorce than are those couples who had not lived together before marriage.[191]

Estimates suggest that 40 percent of children will have lived some time in a cohabiting household by the time they reach age twelve.[192] Many suffer from the instability and family transitions associated with these arrangements. Even when the cohabitants are their biological parents, the children are likely to have to witness the departure of one of them from the household. By age nine, the likelihood of a child with married parents experiencing their breakup is 20 percent. For a child of cohabiting parents, it's 50 percent.[193]

Even among parents with higher education levels, cohabitation is easily twice as unstable as marriage.[194]

Children reared by cohabiting couples are more likely than kids with married parents to engage in delinquent behavior, be suspended from school, and cheat on schoolwork.[195] And when a cohabiting household includes a nonbiologically related male—which is the most common situation[196]—children in the home face dramatically higher risks of sexual and/or physical abuse (compared to children living with their married biological parents).[197] This abuse could even include murder: One Missouri study finds that preschool children living in households with unrelated adults (typically a mother's boyfriend) are nearly fifty times more likely to be killed than are children living with both biological parents.[198] For all these reasons, cohabiting unions are not a good alternative to marriage. They are truly a risk to adults, their relationships, their happiness, and their children.

Same-sex marriage. The crux of the debate over the redefinition of marriage to include homosexual unions has concerned the action's effects on society. And perhaps no area of social-science research has been more contested or politicized than same-sex parenting's effect on child well-being.[199] As we have shown, the larger empirical literature suggests that the two sexes bring different talents to the parenting enterprise, and that children benefit from growing up with both biological parents. We have presented studies concerning the outcomes of adopted children that show adverse effects from the lack of biological connection. Considering the fact that both adoptive and same-sex parents are by definition family configurations that lack the presence of one or both biological parents, it would be reasonable to hypothesize that similar difficulties would be encountered by children in same-sex households. But what has the science actually revealed?

Burgeoning research conducted over the last decade has yielded contradictory findings, concluding a range of positive[200] to neutral[201] to negative[202] effects of same-sex parenting when compared with children of opposite-sex parents. For example, one study found negative effects on school progress and graduation rates,[203] while a similar study did not.[204] In the midst of these ups and downs, however, only eight studies have used a random sample large enough to detect significant differences between outcomes, if they exist, for these two groups of children.[205] Though it is not the case in all of the recent research, several of the large-sample studies find evidence of differential outcomes, including negative impacts on children raised in same-sex parent households.[206] Multiple earlier studies that purported to substantiate the "no differences" perspective[207] were subsequently found to contain coding errors that misclassified children of opposite-sex parents as belonging to the same-sex parent group; when corrected, these studies similarly observe different (more negative) outcomes for the children raised by same-sex couples,[208] across a range of psychological, emotional, and developmental measures.[209] One study found that these children may experience double the risk of emotional problems, for example, misbehavior, poor peer relationships, concentration difficulties, depression, and anxiety, and they were also twice as likely to have received psychological treatment in the past year.[210] These emotional problems persist into adulthood,[211] with one study finding double the incidence of depression at age twenty-eight.[212] Contrary to popular assumptions, children with same-sex parents were found *less* likely to have experienced bullying behavior toward them at school.[213]

While some proponents of same-sex marriage once argued that legal access to marriage would increase positive outcomes for children in these households, some recent studies have shown that certain negative effects actually increase rather than diminish when the same-sex parents are legally married versus cohabiting. For instance, separate studies have noted increases in the number of emotional difficulties[214] and the incidence of sexual abuse.[215]

There is a clear need for ongoing study to better understand these different outcomes for children of same-sex parents. We owe it to the children, their parents, and our fellow scholars to learn what's really happening in this unparalleled social experiment. Strangely, however, selective reporting continues to widely disseminate a misleading picture of the need for further research. One article boldly declared, "The scientific debate over same-sex parenting is over."[216] The article referenced only a single 2016 study that compared ninety-five same-sex and ninety-five opposite-sex households, finding no significant differences in reports of children's health after obtaining a single phone interview with one parent in the household. [217]Some scholars claim that the debate has actually long been settled by a 2005 American Psychological Association brief that has been exposed as blatantly politicized.[218] In no field would science be deemed settled with so little empirical data at such a relatively new stage of inquiry.

For the plenitude of research that *is* being conducted on this topic, various techniques are frequently employed to obscure the true picture, such as using small sample sizes. (Without large numbers of cases, any differences revealed won't be statistically significant enough to report as findings.) In addition, negative outcomes detected may be blamed on the stresses of being part of a minority group (children of same-sex parents), not even considering that they might emerge from the parenting household configuration itself. Finally, married biological parents might be left out entirely as a comparison group,[219] effectively canceling out the greatest contender to a researcher's ideological goals.

Such research methods create increasing tension between objective inquiry and intentional obfuscation of data. In order to further effect cultural change with respect to traditional marriage and family norms, in fact, some family scientists advocate for "queering methodologies" in science. They call on scholars to "move from doing research *on* queer families to doing research *for* (and with) queer families."[220] This research would have the purpose of "correcting systems of oppression," and it would require practitioners of queering methodologies to "effectively disseminate [their] research findings to policymakers and other persons in positions of power."[221]

Independent of these types of political motives, however, the fact remains that same-sex marriage by definition lacks two of the key components that make traditional marriage ideal for children, the first being a biological (genetic) connection with both parents. Stating that children raised in same-sex households are at a disadvantage is based no more on animus toward their parents than when evidence was given showing the same for opposite-sex adoptive parents. Second, same-sex households necessarily lack the dimension of sexual complementarity and undermine the idea that children need both a mother and a father, further weakening the societal norm that men should take responsibility for the children they beget.

The institutional consequences of same-sex marriage run even deeper. Its legalization has corroded marital norms of sexual fidelity, especially as gay male couples tend to downplay the importance of sexual fidelity in their definition of marriage.[222] Redefining marriage as a genderless institution based on adult romantic choices has also further undercut the idea that procreation is intrinsically connected to marriage, and this affects society as a whole.[223] Even prior to *Obergefell*, every U.S. state that had redefined marriage then saw about a 5 percent drop in the opposite-sex marriage rate, compared to the national rate. In 2010, fertility rates were declining nationwide, but states with legalized same-sex marriage saw double the rate of decline than did those without. Then in 2015, same-sex marriage was legalized in all fifty states. Three years later, the U.S. fertility rate has now declined to a historic low for the second year in a row.[224] While these issues are undoubtedly complex, and multiple factors are involved, the fact that drops in fertility consistently correlate with marriage redefinition must be acknowledged. Seen in this light, same-sex marriage is both a consequence of and a further stimulus for the abolition of marriage as the preferred vehicle for ordering sex, procreation, and child rearing. Thus same-sex marriage has further weakened marriage itself at the very moment when it needs to be most strengthened for the good of everyone.

III

Analysis from Philosophy:
The Intrinsic Goods of Marriage

C urrently, there is a battle going on within the sphere of social science concerning marriage (as we define it here) and its benefits compared to various alternatives. However, we remain convinced that the preponderance of objective empirical evidence supports traditional marriage as both an individual and public good. When it comes to the myriad goods of modern social life—economic well-being, safety and security, personal happiness, flourishing community, limited government—marriage is a boon to adults and especially children. But the rational defense of marriage need not be based solely in data about its utility, and those who choose to marry are not usually motivated, first and foremost, by any utilitarian calculus. Only when marriage is valued as good in itself—and not simply as a means to other good ends—will children, adults, and societies reap its profound benefits. This requires defenders of marriage—teachers, poets, religious leaders, parents and grandparents, role models of every kind.

Some moral philosophers have engaged in extended reflection on the nature of marriage as a profound human good, seeking by precise analysis to better understand what most people accept as a matter of common sense. We include this *natural law* perspective here because it represents a view that some thoughtful supporters of marriage find compelling.

Marriage offers spouses a good they can have in no other way: a mutual and complete giving of the self. This act of reciprocal self-giving is made solemn in a mutual promise of exclusive fidelity, a vow to stand by one another as husband and wife amid life's joys and sorrows, and to raise the children that may come as the fruit of this personal, sexual, and familial union. In this way, marriage binds two individuals together for life, and it binds them jointly to the next generation that will follow in their footsteps. Marriage elevates, orders, and at times constrains our natural desires to the higher moral end of fidelity and loving care.

The marriage vow by its nature includes permanence and exclusivity: A couple would lose the very good of the union they seek if they saw their marriage as temporary, or as open to similar sharing with others. What exactly would a temporary promise to love mean? Would it not reduce a person's spouse to a dispensable source of pleasure? To be cared for and kept only so long as the person's own desires are fulfilled? By weakening the permanence of marriage, the contemporary culture of divorce undermines the act of self-giving that is its very foundation. The binding marriage vow is meant to secure some measure of certainty in the face of life's many unknowns—the certainty that whatever trouble comes will not be faced alone. At the same time, their potential offspring receive some measure of protection against becoming mere accessories of someone's lifestyle, to be abandoned or displaced when the parenting partner proves disappointing.

Marriage is by its nature sexual. It gives a unique unitive and procreative meaning to the sexual drive, distinguishing marriage from other close bonds. The emotional, spiritual, and psychological closeness of a married couple is realized in the uniquely biological unity that occurs between them in sexual union; their love is given concrete embodiment. Just as our bodies are not mere instruments of digestion and respiration, our sexual selves are not mere devices of gratification. Male and female are made to relate to and complete one another, to achieve unity in their complementarity. The same act that unites the spouses is also the wellspring of new life. Sharing of lives, then, is also a potential sharing of life itself. In procreation, marital love finds its highest realization and expression. In the family—grounded in a public, prior commitment of mother and father to become one—children find the safety, acceptance, and support they need to reach their full potential.

This deeper understanding of marriage is not narrowly religious. It is the articulation of certain universal truths about human experience, an account of the potential elevation of human nature in marriage that all human beings can rationally grasp. Many nonreligious couples desire these extraordinary things from marriage: permanent and exclusive bonds of love that unite men and women to each other and to their children.

But marriage cannot survive and flourish when the ideal of marriage is eviscerated. Radically different understandings of marriage, now given legal status, have created a culture in which it is much harder if not impossible for people in the United States to grasp the unique benefits that marriage embodies. Maintaining a culture that endorses the good of traditional marriage is essential to ensuring that marriage serves the common good. And in a free society such as our own, a strong marriage culture also fosters liberty by encouraging adults to govern their own lives and rear their children responsibly. But now that same-sex marriage has been legalized, the conjugal conception of marriage—the idea of marriage as a union of sexually complementary spouses—has been abandoned for a consent-based contractual agreement. Such a foundation eliminates, for instance, any principle for limiting the number of partners in a marriage to two. As one mainstream magazine put it the day of the *Obergefell* ruling, "Group marriage is the next horizon."[225]

We now live in a culture in which marriage has all but lost its significance and standing, with children born and reared in a world of post-marital chaos: Anonymous gamete donors can beget thousands without ever knowing their names. Children even of married parents see their friends' lives upended by divorce or de-cohabitation and wonder when *their* number will be up. Ivory tower academics argue for their rights to live sexually unrestrained, while the unions of our poor and less educated citizens flounder in ever-increasing fragility.

Even as we defend the good of marriage as a way of life for individual men and women, we cannot ignore the culture and polity that sustain that way of life. The late Oxford University philosopher Joseph Raz, a self-described liberal, was rightly critical of those forms of liberalism which suppose that law and government can and should be neutral with respect to competing conceptions of moral goodness. As he put it, "Monogamy, assuming that it is the only valuable form of marriage, cannot be practiced by an individual. It requires a culture which recognizes it, and which supports it through the public's attitude and through its formal institutions."[226]

If monogamy is indeed a key element in a sound understanding of marriage, then this ideal needs to be preserved and promoted in law and in policy. Yet the opposite has been done. Our primary institutions, including universities, courts, legislatures, and some religious institutions, have now redefined marriage legally, conceptually, and in practice. Many young people will never learn what it means to get and stay married, to live in fidelity to and peace with the spouse they choose and the children to whom they must be devoted. The law is a teacher, instructing either that marriage is a reality whose contours individuals cannot remake at will, or that marriage is a mere convention—so malleable that individuals, couples, or groups can choose to make of it whatever suits their desires of the moment. Currently, U.S. law teaches the latter, to the detriment of us all.

Moreover, a hostile environment now exists where supporters of traditional marriage are not free to live out their beliefs and convictions without being falsely labeled as bigoted and backwards. Cultural and government forces seek to impose a new sexual orthodoxy—tolerating no dissent—upon any who retain principled support for the superiority of the traditional norm.[227]

IV

America's Way Forward: Eight Actions

When it comes to family life, the great paradox of our time is this: Every society that we think of as generally best for human flourishing—stable, democratic, developed, and free—is experiencing a radical crisis around human generativity. Family fragmentation and fatherlessness are increasing enormously, usually coupled with the collapse of fertility to levels that, if continued, spell demographic and social decline. Suddenly, developed nations are finding themselves unable to accomplish the great, simple task of every human society: bringing young men and women together to marry and raise the next generation together. With legalized same-sex marriage and historically low marriage and fertility rates, the United States has accelerated its own descent into this state of affairs. For the first time in our nation's history, older people are projected to outnumber children by the year 2030.[228] In the face of decline, however, we are witnessing a "marriage movement" and pockets of reasoned resistance. The great task for America in our generation is to energize a return to and renewal of traditional marriage. We need to transmit a stronger, healthier, and more supportive marriage culture to the next generation, so that each year more children are raised by their own mother and father united by a loving marriage, so that they can grow up to have thriving marriages themselves.

Our task is a daunting one. Creating such a marriage culture is not the job for government, and in numerous instances, the government has now declared open hostility toward many who would seek to do so.[229] Nevertheless, families, religious communities, and civic institutions, along with intellectual, moral, religious, and artistic leaders, must dare to point the way. We call upon our nation's leaders and our fellow citizens to support public policies that strengthen traditional marriage as a social institution. This nation must reestablish the normative understanding of marriage as the union—intended for life—of a man and a woman, who welcome and raise together any children who are the fruit of their self-giving love, extending the family tree into a flourishing grove where other citizens can rest in its shade.

In particular, we single out eight actions toward undergirding and strengthening marriage:

1. Maintain the legal distinction between married and cohabiting couples. Powerful intellectual institutions in family law, including the American Law Institute, have proposed that America follow the path of many European nations and Canada in erasing the legal distinction between marriage and cohabitation. But such a shift in law would create further harm by sending a false message to the next generation that marriage itself is irrelevant or secondary, thus we encourage our legislators to refuse to extend legal marital status to cohabiting couples. We believe it is unjust as well as unwise to either (a) impose marital obligations on people who have not consented to them or (b) extend marital benefits to couples who have not promised marital responsibilities.

2. Investigate divorce-law reforms. Under America's current divorce system, courts today provide less protection for the marriage contract than they do for an ordinary business contract. Some of us support a return to a fault-based divorce system; others of us do not. But all of us recognize that the current system is a failure in both practical and moral terms, and deeply in need of reform. We call for renewed efforts to discover ways in which laws can strengthen marriage and reduce unnecessarily high rates of divorce. We affirm that protecting U.S. persons from domestic violence and abuse is a critically important goal. But because both children and adults in nonmarital unions are at vastly increased risk for both, encouraging high rates of family fragmentation is not a good strategy for protecting them. Proposals we consider worthy of more consideration include the following:

- **Extend waiting periods for unilateral no-fault divorce.** Require couples in nonviolent marriages to attend (religious, secular, or public) counseling designed to resolve their differences and renew their marital vows.

- **Permit the creation of prenuptial covenants that restrict divorce** for couples who seek more extensive marriage commitments than current laws allow. (The enforcement by secular courts of Orthodox Jewish marriage contracts may provide a useful model, as well as Louisiana's "Covenant Marriage" option.)

- **Expand court-connected divorce-education programs to include divorce interventions** (such as PAIRS[230] or Retrouvaille[231]) that help facilitate reconciliations as well as reduce acrimony and litigation.

- **Apply standards of fault to the distribution of property, where consistent with the best interests of children.** Spouses who are abusive or unfaithful should not share marital property equally with innocent spouses. The laments of spouses whose mate has left them against their will—especially in order to form a new union—ought to be heard and considered.

- **Create pilot programs on marriage education and divorce interventions in high-risk communities,** using both faith-based and secular programs. Track program effectiveness to establish "best practices" that could be replicated elsewhere.[232]

3. End marriage penalties for low-income Americans. To address the growing racial and class divisions in marriage, federal and state governments ought to act quickly to eliminate the marriage penalties embedded in means-tested welfare and tax policies—such as the Earned Income Tax Credit (EITC) and Medicaid—that affect couples with low and moderate incomes.[233] A recent study found that where there was an anticipated loss of income-tax credit due to a marriage penalty, lower-income women were less likely to marry and more likely to cohabit; thus, financial disincentives are potentially affecting the marriage decisions of millions of low-income women.[234] It is unconscionable that government levies substantial financial penalties on low-income parents who marry. Other approaches to strengthening marriage for couples and communities at risk include public information campaigns, marriage education programs, and jobs programs for low-income couples who wish to get and stay married. Experimenting with such new initiatives allows scholars to determine which measures are best suited to the task at hand.[235]

4. Protect and expand prochild and profamily provisions in our tax code. The tax code ought to privilege institutions that stabilize society and help those making sacrifices to ensure the next generation.

5. Protect the interests of children against a powerful fertility industry. Treating the making of babies as a business like any other is fundamentally inconsistent with the dignity of human persons and the human rights of children. We urge Americans to consider the following proposals:

- **Ban the use of anonymous sperm and egg donation for all adults.** Children have a right to know their biological origins. Adults have no right to strip children of this knowledge to satisfy their own desires for a family. Countries such as the Netherlands, Norway, Sweden, Switzerland, Finland, New Zealand, and the UK all have banned this practice to protect the identity rights of donor-conceived children.[236]

- **Ban all surrogacy.** Some countries, such as Thailand and India, have banned commercial surrogacy; others, such as Nepal and Sweden, have banned all surrogacy. The European Parliament has condemned surrogacy as "reproductive exploitation" that "undermines the human dignity" of women, particularly "vulnerable women in developing countries."[237] Surrogacy also commodifies the children being carried, subjects them to increased health risks, and disregards their rights by prioritizing adult desire over a child's best interests.[238]

- **Consider restricting reproductive technologies to married couples.**

- **Refuse to create legally fatherless children.**
  Require men who are sperm donors (and/or the clinics that trade in gametes) to retain legal and financial responsibility for any children they create who lack a legal father. The most important forces underwriting the current United States fertility industry are not technological; they are social and legal. Both law and culture have stressed the interests of adults to the exclusion of the needs of children. Parents seeking children deserve our sympathy and support. But we ought not, in offering this, deliberately create an entire class of children deprived of their natural human right to know their own origins and to experience the unique love of both a mother and a father.

6. Protect the freedom to live out and express belief in the uniqueness of traditional marriage without fear of government coercion and institutional hostility. Instances of intolerance for individuals who hold a traditional view of marriage grow more numerous by the day and are increasingly accompanied by legal efforts to compel either violations of individual conscience or religious beliefs.[239] For instance, faith-based adoption and foster-care providers have been forced to compromise their belief that placing children in homes with a mother and a father is in the best interest of the child—or to cease offering services entirely, leaving vulnerable children in need.[240]

Among the most well-known cases of religious harassment is that of baker Jack Phillips, who after declining to create a wedding cake for a same-sex ceremony, was pursued by the state of Colorado in a case that ultimately went to the Supreme Court. In June 2018, the Court ruled that the Colorado Civil Rights Commission had acted with hostility toward Phillips based on his religious beliefs.[241] Less than a month after the Supreme Court ruled in his favor, the same Colorado Commission found probable cause against Phillips for declining to create a cake celebrating an individual's gender transition.[242] In a similar way, sexual orientation and gender identity (SOGI) nondiscrimination laws are often used by their backers as a sword "to punish the wicked," as multimillionaire activist Tim Gill refers to his goals for such laws.[243] We can only interpret this kind of language to indicate an intention to silence and stamp out dissent, violating legitimate individual and religious liberty.[244]

7. Protect the freedom to conduct scholarly inquiry and promote dissemination of accurate research findings on marriage and related topics. In tandem with the widespread misrepresentation of research findings both in academia and public media on the subject of marriage, a disturbing trend toward actual suppression of research based on ideological rather than scientific grounds appears to be emerging and altering the playing field in the study of sexuality and gender. For example, in August 2018, Brown University assistant professor Lisa Littman published a study that explored the recent statistical upsurge of adolescent and young-adult gender-dysphoric girls and the possibility of social media and peer influence as a contributing factor.[245] Despite being peer reviewed and found acceptable, the study was immediately denounced online by transsexual activists, since it suggested that some of the girls could have been influenced by forces outside of themselves. In response to the attacks, the journal editors posted a comment of concern and began an inquiry and additional review.[246] Brown University took down their original promotional article about Littman's study and removed it from their news distribution in what they called "the most responsible course of action."[247] Their reasoning was not that the study was faulty but that it "could be used to discredit efforts to support transgender youth."[248] A former dean of Harvard Medical School spoke out against the journal's and Brown's actions,[249] as did many of the parents who had actually participated in Littman's study.[250]

8. Restore the public understanding of marriage as uniquely the union of one man with one woman as husband and wife. In 2015, five Supreme Court justices redefined marriage and imposed a new legal standard of what marriage means, with some of them erroneously declaring that our historic understanding of marriage as the union of one man and one woman is rooted in animus or ignorance. While these legal mandates won't be easily reversed, we can seek to restore the public's understanding of the unique goods of traditional marriage for society. Our best hope is to foster a nonpartisan cultural renewal (which admittedly will take decades) so that a new generation of legislators and justices will arise to legally reestablish the institution of marriage for the good of all Americans. Families, religious communities, community organizations, and public policymakers must work together toward a great goal: strengthening marriage so that each year more children are raised by their own mother and father in loving, lasting marital unions. The survival of the American experiment depends upon it. And our children deserve nothing less.

Notes

1   David Popenoe. 1988. Third printing 2012. *Disturbing the Nest: Family Change and Decline in Modern Societies*. New Brunswick, NJ: Aldine Transaction; Alan Wolfe. 1989. *Whose Keeper? Social Science and Moral Obligation*. Berkeley: University of California Press.

2   Brienna Perelli-Harris, Ann Berrington, Nora Sánchez Gassen, Paulina Galezewska, and Jennifer A. Holland. 2017. "The Rise in Divorce and Cohabitation: Is There a Link?" *Population and Development Review* 43 (2): 303–329. https://doi.org/10.1111/padr.12063.

3   Ryan T. Anderson. 2015. *Truth Overruled*. Washington, DC: Regnery Publishing.

4   Frank Bruni. 2015. "Bigotry, the Bible, and the Lessons of Indiana." *New York Times* April 3. https://www.nytimes.com/2015/04/05/opinion/sunday/frank-bruni-same-sex-sinners.html.

5   W. Bradford Wilcox and Nicholas H. Wolfinger. 2016. *Soul Mates: Religion, Sex, Love, and Marriage among African Americans and Latinos*. New York: Oxford University Press; W. Bradford Wilcox and Steven L. Nock. 2006. "What's Love Got to Do with It? Ideology, Equity, Gender, and Women's Marital Happiness." *Social Forces* 84: 1321–1345; Vaughn R.A. Call and Tim B. Heaton. 1997. "Religious Influence on Marital Stability." *Journal for the Scientific Study of Religion* 36: 382–392.

6   W. Bradford Wilcox *et al.* 2011. *Why Marriage Matters, Third Edition: Thirty Conclusions from the Social Sciences*. New York: Institute for American Values.

7   Kristin Anderson Moore, Susan M. Jekielek, and Carol Emig 2002. "Marriage from a Child's Perspective: How Does Family Structure Affect Children, and What Can Be Done about It?" *Research Brief, June*. Washington, DC: Child Trends. P. 6.

8   For summaries from Brookings and Princeton, see Sara McLanahan, Elisabeth Donahue, and Ron Haskins. 2005. "Introducing the Issue." *The Future of Children* 15: 3–12. For the Center for Law and Social Policy's statement, see Mary Parke. 2003. *Are Married Parents Really Better for Children?* Washington, DC: Center for Law and Social Policy. For the Institute for American Values's statement, see Wilcox *et al.* 2011.

9   Anderson. 2015. P. 152.

10   Margaret A. Keyes, Anu Sharma, Irene J. Elkins, William G. Iacono, and Matt McGue. 2008. "The Mental Health of U.S. Adolescents Adopted in Infancy." *Archives of Pediatrics & Adolescent Medicine* 162(5): 419–425.

11   Nicholas Zill and W. Bradford Wilcox. 2018. "The Adoptive Difference: New Evidence on How Adopted Children Perform in School." *Research Brief, March* . Charlottesville, VA: Institute for Family Studies. https://ifstudies.org/blog/the-adoptive-difference-new-evidence-on-how-adopted-children-perform-in-school. Nicholas Zill. 2015. "The Paradox of Adoption." *Research Brief, October.* Charlottesville, VA: Institute for Family Studies. https://ifstudies.org/blog/the-paradox-of-adoption.

12   Margaret A. Keyes, Stephen M. Malone, Anu Sharma, William G. Iacono, and Matt McGue. 2013. "Risk of Suicide Attempt in Adopted and Non-adopted Offspring." *Pediatrics* 1 32(4): 639–646. See also Gail Slap, Elizabeth Goodman, and Bin Huang. 2001. "Adoption as a Risk Factor for Attempted Suicide During Adolescence." *Pediatrics* 108(2): e30.

13   Daniel E. Shumer, Aser Abrha, Henry A. Feldman, and Jeremi Carswell. "Overrepresentation of Adopted Adolescents at a Hospital-Based Gender Dysphoria Clinic." *Transgender Health* 2(1). https://doi.org/10.1089/trgh.2016.0042.

14   Kathleen Kingsbury. 2008. "Adoptees More Likely to Be Troubled." *Time* May 5. http://content.time.com/time/health/article/0,8599,1737667,00.html.

15   Kyle Pruett. 2000. *Fatherneed.* New York: Broadway. P. 207. See also Elizabeth Marquardt. 2005a. *Between Two Worlds: The Inner Lives of Children of Divorce.* New York: Crown; David Popenoe. 1996. *Life Without Father.* Cambridge, MA: Harvard University Press.

16   Elizabeth Marquardt, Norval D. Glenn, and Karen Clark. 2010. *My Daddy's Name is Donor: A New Study of Young Adults Conceived through Sperm Donation.* New York: Institute for American Values.

17   Pruett. 2000. Pp. 204–208. Various recent studies contest these difficulties, claiming that the well-being of donor-conceived children is not affected by the lack of biological connection. For example, a 2013 study diminished the importance of a genetic connection when it concluded that the psychological adjustment of donor-conceived children was similar to that of naturally conceived children. However, the study was based on subjective rather than objective measures and relied on maternal reports (and some additional teacher reports) of the children's well-being at ages three, seven, and ten years. At best, the study design was quite limited; objective, long-term effects were not measured. Additionally, the study acknowledged the limitation that mothers might underreport difficulties due to a desire to validate their reproductive choices. Yet the findings are offered as evidence for the alleged insignificance of biological connections. See Susan Golombok, Lucy Blake, Polly Casey, Gabriela Roman, and Vasanti Jadva. 2013. "Children Born through Reproductive Donation: A Longitudinal Study of Psychological Adjustment." *Journal of Child Psychology, Psychiatry, and Allied Disciplines* 54(6): 653–660. Due to increased problems reported for the children born via surrogacy, this study conceded that the lack of a gestational connection might have a negative impact on the child and thus hypothesized that a gestational connection might be more important than a genetic one.

18   For example, see Alana S. Newman. 2014. *The Anonymous Us Project.* New York: Broadway Publications; Alana S. Newman. 2016. *Anonymous Us Volume 2.* Independently published. See also https://anonymousus.org for a growing database ("story collective") of personal accounts from those affected by third-party reproduction.

19   Wendy Kramer. 2016. "Sperm and Egg Donation: Ten Things Your Doctor, Clinic, or Sperm Bank Won't Tell You." *Huffington Post* December 4. https://www.huffpost.com/entry/sperm-egg-donation-10-things-your-doctor-clinic_b_582dd81 5e4b08c963e343bca.

20   Paul Raeburn. 2014. *Do Fathers Matter? What Science Is Telling Us about the Parent We've Overlooked.* New York: Scientific American/Farrar, Straus, and Giroux.

21   Amina P. Alio *et al.* 2011. "Assessing the Impact of Paternal Involvement on Racial/Ethnic Disparities in Infant Mortality Rates." *Journal of Community Health* 36(1): 63–68. https://doi.org/10.1007/s10900-010-9280-3.

22   James A. Gaudino, Bill Jenkins, and Roger W. Rochat. 1999. "No Fathers' Names: A Risk Factor for Infant Mortality in the State of Georgia, USA." *Social Science & Medicine* 48(2): 253–260.

23   Gregory D. Webster, Julia A. Graber, Amanda N. Gesselman, Benjamin S. Crosier, and Tatiana Orozco Schember. 2014. "A Life History Theory of Father Absence and Menarche: A Meta-analysis." *Evolutionary Psychology* 12: 273–294. https://doi.org/10.1177/147470491401200202.

24   Amana C. La Guardia, Judith A. Nelson, and Ian M. Lertora. 2014. "The Impact of Father Absence on Daughter Sexual Development and Behaviors: Implications for Professional Counselors." *Family Journal* 22(3): 339–346.

25   Danielle J. DelPriore, Gabriel L. Schlomer, and Bruce J. Ellis. 2017. "Impact of Fathers on Parental Monitoring of Daughters and their Affiliation with Sexually Promiscuous Peers: A Genetically and Environmentally Controlled Sibling Study." *Developmental Psychology* 53(7): 1330–1343.

26   Jessica A. Hehman and Catherine A. Salmon. 2018. "Sex-specific Developmental Effects of Father Absence on Casual Sexual Behavior and Life History Strategy." *Evolutionary Psychological Science*, September. https://doi.org/10.1007/s40806-018-0173-5.

27   Sara McLanahan and Gary Sandefur. 1994. *Growing Up with a Single Parent.* Cambridge, MA: Harvard University Press; Bruce Ellis *et al.* 2003. "Does Father Absence Place Daughters at Special Risk for Early Sexual Activity and Teenage Pregnancy?" *Child Development* 7 4: 801–821.

28   Ellis *et al.* 2003.

29   Wilcox *et al.* 2011.

30   Andrea J. Sedlak *et al.* 2010. *Fourth National Incidence Study of Child Abuse and Neglect (NIS–4): Report to Congress.* Washington, DC: U.S. Department of Health and Human Services, Administration for Children and Families.

31   Anne Case *et al.* 2000. "How Hungry is the Selfish Gene?" *Economic Journal* 110: 781–804; Wilcox *et al.* 2011; Jacinta Bronte-Tinkew, Allison Horowitz, and Mindy E. Scott. 2009. "Fathering with Multiple Partners: Links to Children's Well-being in Early Childhood." *Journal of Marriage and Family* 7 1(3): 608–31; Sara S. McLanahan. 2011. "Family Instability and Complexity after a Nonmarital Birth: Outcomes for Children in Fragile Families." In M. J. Carlson and P. England, Eds. *Social Class and Changing Families in an Unequal America.* Stanford, CT: Stanford University Press. Pp.1–20.

32   Wendy Sigle-Rushton and Sarah S. McLanahan. 2004. "Father Absence and Child Wellbeing: A Critical Review." In D. P. Moynihan, T. M. Smeeding, and L. Rainwater, Eds. *The Future of the Family.* New York: Russell Sage. Pp. 116–155; Andrew Cherlin. 1978. "Remarriage as an Incomplete Institution." *American Journal of Sociology* 84(3): 634–50.

33   Wilcox *et al*. 2011; Donna Ginther and Robert Pollak. 2004. "Family Structure and Children's Educational Outcomes: Blended Families, Stylized Facts, and Descriptive Regressions." *Demography* 41(4): 671–96; Sarah Halpern-Meekin and Laura Tach. 2008. "Heterogeneity in Two-Parent Families and Adolescent Well-Being." *Journal of Marriage and Family* 70(2): 435–51; Lisa A. Gennetian. 2005. "One or Two Parents? Half or Step Siblings? The Effects of Family Composition on Young Children's Achievement." *Journal of Population Economics* 18(3): 415–436.

34   Andrew J. Cherlin. 2010. *The Marriage-Go-Round: The State of Marriage and the Family in America Today.* New York: Vintage Books. P. 6.

35   Sara McLanahan, Laura Tach, and Daniel Schneider. 2013. "The Causal Effects of Father Absence." *Annual Review of Sociology* 39: 399-427. https://doi.org/10.1146/annurev-soc-071312-145704.

36   Ross Parke. 1996. *Fatherhood*. Cambridge, MA: Harvard University Press. P.101.

37   Sandra Hofferth and Kermyt Anderson. 2003. "Are All Dads Equal? Biology Versus Marriage as a Basis for Paternal Involvement." *Journal of Marriage and Family* 6 5: 213–232; Wilcox *et al*. 2011.

38   Valarie King and Holly Heard. 1999. "Nonresident Father Visitation, Parental Conflict, and Mother's Satisfaction: What's Best for Child Well-being?" *Journal of Marriage and Family* 61: 385–396; Elaine Sorenson and Chava Zibman. 2000. *To What Extent Do Children Benefit from Child Support?* Washington, DC: The Urban Institute.

39   Raeburn. 2014. P. 221.

40   Paul Amato. 1998. "More Than Money? Men's Contributions to Their Children's Lives." In A. Booth and A.C. Crouter, Eds. *Men in Families: When Do They Get Involved? What Difference Does It Make?* Mahwah, NJ: Lawrence Erlbaum Associates; Jay Belsky, Lise Youngblade, Michael Rovine, and Brenda Volling. 1991. "Patterns of Marital Change and Parent-Child Interaction." *Journal of Marriage and Family* 5 3: 487–498; Wilcox *et al*. 2011.

41   Raeburn. 2014. P. 234.

42   Ross D. Parke. 2013. "Gender Differences and Similarities in Parental Behavior." In W. B. Wilcox and K. K. Kline, Eds. *Gender and Parenthood: Biological and Social Scientific Perspectives*. New York: Columbia University Press. Pp. 120–163.

43   Eleanor Maccoby. 1998. *The Two Sexes: Growing Up Apart, Coming Together.* Cambridge, MA: Harvard University.

44   David Geary. 1998. *Male, Female: The Evolution of Human Sex Differences.* Washington, DC: American Psychological Association. P. 104.

45   Wade Horn and Tom Sylvester. 2002. *Father Facts.* Gaithersburg, MD: National Fatherhood Initiative. P.153; Popenoe. 1996. P. 145; Thomas G. Powers *et al.* 1994. "Compliance and Self-Assertion: Young Children's Responses to Mothers Versus Fathers." Developmental Psychology 30: 980–989.

46   Kevin MacDonald and Ross D. Parke. 1986. "Parent-Child Physical Play: The Effects of Sex and Age of Children and Parents." *Sex Roles* 78: 367–379; Thomas G. Power and Ross D. Parke. 1982. "Play as a Context for Early Learning: Lab and Home Analyses." In L. M. Laosa and I. E. Sigel, Eds. *The Family as a Learning Environment.* New York: Plenum. Pp. 147–178.

47   Pruett. 2000. Pp. 30–31; Popenoe. 1996. Pp. 144–145.

48   Geary. 1998. P. 142.

49   Nadya Pancsofar and Lynne Vernon-Feagans. 2010. "Fathers' Early Contributions to Children's Language Development in Families from Low-Income Rural Communities." *Early Childhood Research Quarterly* 25(4): 450–463.

50   Marie Arsalidou, Emmanuel J. Barbeau, Sarah J. Bayless, and Margot J. Taylor. 2010. "Brain Responses Differ to Faces of Mothers and Fathers." *Brain and Cognition* 74: 47–51.

51   Marquardt. 2005a; Paul Amato. 2005. "The Impact of Family Formation Change on the Cognitive, Social, and Emotional Well-being of the Next Generation." *The Future of Children* 15: 75–96.

52   Paul G. Ramchandani *et al.* 2012. "Do Early Father-Infant Interactions Predict the Onset of Externalising Behaviours in Young Children? Findings from a Longitudinal Cohort Study." *Journal of Child Psychology and Psychiatry and Allied Disciplines* 54 (1): 56–64.

53   Cynthia Harper and Sara McLanahan. 2004. "Father Absence and Youth Incarceration." *Journal of Research on Adolescence* 14: 369–397.

54   Melanie H. Mallers, Susan T. Charles, Shevaun D. Neupert, and David M. Almeida. 2010. "Perceptions of Childhood Relationships with Mother and Father: Daily Emotional and Stressor Experiences in Adulthood." *Developmental Psychology* 46 (6): 1651–1661.

55   Harper and McLanahan. 2004.

56   Brian D'Onofrio *et al.* 2006. "A Genetically Informed Study of the Processes Underlying the Association between Parental Marital Instability and Offspring Adjustment." *Developmental Psychology* 42(3): 486–499; Brian D'Onofrio *et al.* 2005. "A Genetically Informed Study of Marital Instability and Its Association with Offspring Psychopathology." *Journal of Abnormal Psychology* 114: 570–586.

57   Elizabeth Marquardt. 2005b. *Family Structure and Children's Educational Outcomes*. New York: Institute for American Values.

58   Julie E. Artis. 2007. "Maternal Cohabitation and Child Well-being among Kindergarten Children." *Journal of Marriage and Family* 6 9(1): 222–36.

59   Marquardt. 2005b.

60   McLanahan and Sandefur. 1994.

61   R. Kelly Raley, Michelle L. Frisco, and Elizabeth Wildsmith. 2005. "Maternal Cohabitation and Educational Success." *Sociology of Education* 7 8(2): 14464.

62   Camron S. Devor, Susan D. Stewart, and Cassandra Dorius. 2018. "Parental Divorce, Social Capital, and Postbaccalaurate Educational Attainment among Young Adults." *Journal of Family Issues* 39(10): 2806–35. https://doi. org/10.1177/0192513X18760349.

63   Robert I. Lerman, Joseph Price, and W. Bradford Wilcox. 2017. "Family Structure and Economic Success across the Life Course." *Marriage & Family Review* 53(8): 744–758. https://doi.org/10.1080/01494929.2017.1316810.

64   Fabrizio Bernardi, Diederik Boertien, and Koen Geven. 2019. "Childhood Family Structure and the Accumulation of Wealth across the Life Course." *Journal of Marriage and Family* 8 1(1): 230–247. https://doi.org/10.1111/jomf.12523.

65   Wilcox *et al*. 2011. Marquardt. 2005a.

66   Gunilla Ringback Weitoft, Anders Hjern, Bengt Haglund, and Mans Rosen. 2003. "Mortality, Severe Morbidity, and Injury in Children Living with Single Parents in Sweden: A Population-based Study." *Lancet* 3 61: 289–295.

67   Sara McLanahan. 1997. "Parent Absence or Poverty: Which Matters More?" In G. Duncan and J. Brooks-Gunn, Eds. *Consequences of Growing Up Poor*. New York: Russell Sage.

68   Wilcox *et al*. 2011; McLanahan and Sandefur. 1994.

69   Wilcox *et al*. 2011; Popenoe. 1996.

70   Hofferth and Anderson. 2003; Wilcox *et al*. 2011.

71   Alysse ElHage. 2016. "Why I Choose the 'Gold Standard' of Family Forms." *Institute for Family Studies Blog*, September 21. https://ifstudies.org/blog/why-i-choose-the-gold-standard-of-family-forms.

72   Linda Waite and Maggie Gallagher. 2000. *The Case for Marriage*. New York: Doubleday.

73   *Ibid*.

74   Joseph Lupton and James P. Smith. 2003."Marriage, Assets and Savings." In S. A. Grossbard-Schectman, Ed. *Marriage and the Economy: Theories from Advanced Industrial Societies.* Cambridge and New York: Cambridge University Press; Janet Wilmoth and Gregor Koso. 2002. "Does Marital History Matter? Marital Status and Wealth Outcomes among Preretirement Adults." *Journal of Marriage and Family* 64(1): 254–268; Lingxin Hao. 1996. "Family Structure, Private Transfers, and the Economic Well-being of Families with Children." *Social Forces* 75(1): 269–92; Lucie Schmidt and Purvi Sevak. 2006. "Gender, Marriage, and Asset Accumulation in the United States." *Feminist Economics* 12(1–2): 139–166; Wilcox *et al.* 2011; W. Bradford Wilcox and Joseph Price. 2018. "Families and the Wealth of Nations." In N. Cahn, J. Carbone, L. F. DeRose, and W. B. Wilcox, Eds. *Unequal Family Lives: Causes and Consequences in Europe and the Americas.* New York: Cambridge University Press.

75   David Popenoe and Barbara Dafoe Whitehead. 2005. *The State of Our Unions.* New Brunswick, NJ: National Marriage Project.

76   Nicholas Eberstadt. 2018. "Family Structure and the Decline of Work for Men in Postwar America." In N. Cahn, J. Carbone, L. F. DeRose, and W. B. Wilcox, Eds. *Unequal Family Lives: Causes and Consequences in Europe and the Americas.* New York: Cambridge University Press; Nicholas Eberstadt. 2016. *Men Without Work: America's Invisible Crisis.* Conshohocken PA: Templeton.

77   Michelle J. Budig and Paula England. 2001. "The Wage Penalty for Motherhood." *American Sociological Review* 66: 204–225.

78   W. Bradford Wilcox, Wendy R. Wang, and Ronald B. Mincy. 2018. "Black Men Making It in America: The Engines of Economic Success for Black Men in America." *Research Brief, June.* American Enterprise Institute and Institute for Family Studies.

79   W. Bradford Wilcox and Robert I. Lerman. 2014. "For Richer, For Poorer: How Family Structures Economic Success in America." *Research Brief, October.* American Enterprise Institute and Institute for Family Studies.

80   *Ibid.*

81   Robert I. Lerman. 2002a. "Impacts of Marital Status and Parental Presence on the Material Hardship of Families with Children." *Research Brief, July.* W ashington, DC: Urban Institute. https://www.urban.org/sites/default/files/publication/60501/410538-Impacts-of-Marital-Status-and-Parental-Presence-on-the-Material-Hardship-of-Families-with-Children.PDF; Robert I. Lerman. 2002b. "Married and Unmarried Parenthood and Economic Well-Being: A Dynamic Analysis of a Recent Cohort." *Research Brief.* Washington, DC: Urban Institute. http://webarchive.urban.org/UploadedPDF/410540_Parenthood.pdf; Daniel

T. Lichter, Deborah Roempke Graefe, and J. Brian Brown. 2003. "Is Marriage a Panacea? Union Formation among Economically Disadvantaged Unwed Mothers." *Social Problems* 5 0(1): 60–86.

82 Wilcox and Price. 2018.

83 *Ibid.* P. 195.

84 Susan Martinuk. 2016. "Marriage Is Good For Your Health." *Research Brief, September.* Hamilton, Ontario, Canada: Cardus.

85 *Ibid.*

86 Ayal A. Aizer *et al.* 2013. "Marital Status and Survival in Patients with Cancer." *Journal of Clinical Oncology* 4 9: 3869–76; David W. Kissane. 2013. "Marriage Is as Protective as Chemotherapy." *Journal of Clinical Oncology* 51: 5080.

87 Ellen L. Idler, David A. Boulifard, and Richard J. Contrada. 2012. "Mending Broken Hearts: Marriage and Mortality following Cardiac Surgery." *Journal of Health and Social Behavior* 53(1): 33–49. https://doi.org/10.1177/0022146511432342.

88 David J. Roelfs, Eran Shor, Rachel Kalish, and Tamar Yogev. 2011. "The Rising Relative Risk of Mortality for Singles: Meta-analysis and Meta-regression." *American Journal of Epidemiology* 1 74(4): 379–89. https://doi.org/10.1093/aje/kwr111.

89 Lamberto Manzoli, Paolo Villari, Giovanni M. Pirone, and Antonio Boccia. 2007. "Marital Status and Mortality in the Elderly: A Systematic Review and Meta-analysis." *Social Science and Medicine* 6 4(1): 77–94. https://doi.org/10.1016/j.socscimed.2006.08.031.

90 Michael S. Rendall, Margaret M. Weden, Melissa M. Favreault, and Hilary Waldron. 2011. "The Protective Effect of Marriage for Survival: A Review and Update." *Demography* 48: 481–506.

91 Shawn Grover and John F. Helliwell. 2017. "How's Life at Home? New Evidence on Marriage and the Set Point for Happiness." *Journal of Happiness Studies.* https://doi.org/10.1007/s10902-017-9941-3; Paul R. Amato. 2015. "Marriage, Cohabitation and Mental Health." *Family Matters* 96: 5–13; Waite and Gallagher. 2000; Steven Stack and J. Ross Eshleman. 1998. "Marital Status and Happiness: A Seventeen-Nation Study." *Journal of Marriage and Family* 60: 527–36.

92 Jim P. Stimpson, Fernando A. Wilson, Shinobu Watanbe-Galloway, and M. Kristen Peek. 2012. "The Effect of Marriage on Utilization of Colorectal Endoscopy Exam in the United States." *International Journal of Cancer Epidemiology, Detection and Prevention* 36(5): e325–e332.

93   Rendall, Weden, Favreault, and Waldron. 2011; Waite and Gallagher. 2000; Inez
     M. A. Juong, Jacobus J. Glerum, Frans W. A. Van Poppel, Jan W. P. F. Kardaun,
     and Johan P Mackenbach. 1996. "The Contribution of Specific Causes of Death
     to Mortality Differences by Marital Status in the Netherlands." *European Journal
     of Public Health* 6(2): 142–149; Walter R. Gove. 1973. "Sex, Marital Status and
     Mortality." *American Journal of Sociology* 79: 45–67.

94   Jana Staton. 2008. "What Is the Relationship of Marriage to Physical Health?" *Fact
     Sheet.* Oklahoma City, OK: National Healthy Marriage Resource Center; Robert
     G. Wood, Brian Goesling, and Sarah Avellar. 2007. "The Effects of Marriage on
     Health: A Synthesis of Recent Research Evidence." *Research Brief.* Princeton, NJ:
     Mathematica Policy Research.

95   Jonathan Scourfield and Rhiannon Evans. 2015. "Why Might Men Be
     More at Risk of Suicide after a Relationship Breakdown? Sociological
     Insights." *American Journal of Men's Health* September: 380–84. https://doi.
     org/10.1177/1557988314546395.

96   Janice K. Kiecolt-Glaser, Jean-Philippe Gouin, and Liisa Hantsoo. 2010. "Close
     Relationships, Inflammation and Health." *Neuroscience & Biobehavioral Review*
     35: 33–38; James A. Coan, Hillary S. Schaefer, and Richard J. Davidson.
     2006. "Lending a Hand: Social Regulation of the Neural Response to Threat."
     Psychological Science 1 7(12): 1032–39; Waite and Gallagher. 2000.

97   Theodore F. Robles and Janice K. Kiecolt-Glaser. 2003. "The Physiology of
     Marriage: Pathways to Health." *Physiology and Behavior* 79: 409–16; Sue M.
     Johnson *et al.* 2013. "Soothing the Threatened Brain: Leveraging Contact Comfort
     with Emotionally Focused Therapy." *PLOS ONE* 8(11): e79314. https://doi.
     org/10.1371/journal.pone.0079314.

98   Martinuk. 2016.

99   Charlotte A. Schoenborn. 2004. "Marital Status and Health: United States,
     1999–2002." *Advance Data from Vital and Health Statistics 351.* Hyattsville, MD:
     National Center for Health Statistics. https://pdfs.semanticscholar.org/9b35/
     f4dcaa1831e05adda9a8e37e6d590c79609b.pdf.

100 Kate Lunau. 2014. "How Marriage Can Save Your Life." *Maclean's* January 9.
     https://www.macleans.ca/society/health/how-marriage-can-save-your-life.

101 Mioara Zoutewelle-Terovan, Victor van der Geest, Aart Liefbroer, and Catrien
     Bijleveld. "Criminality and Family Formation: Effects of Marriage and Parenthood
     on Criminal Behavior for Men and Women." *Crime & Delinquency* 60(8):
     1209–1234. https://doi.org/10.1177/0011128712441745; Kenneth S. Kendler,

S. L. Lönn, J. Sundquist, and K. Sundquist. 2017. "The Role of Marriage in Criminal Recidivism: A Longitudinal and Co-relative Analysis." *Epidemiology and Psychiatric Sciences* 26(6): 655–63.

102 Michelle L. Frisco, Marin R. Wenger, and Derek A. Kreager. 2016. "Extradyadic Sex and Union Dissolution among Young Adults in Opposite-sex Married and Cohabiting Unions." *Social Science Research 62*: 291–304; Waite and Gallagher. 2000; Judith Treas and Deirdre Giesen. 2000. "Sexual Infidelity among Married and Cohabiting Americans." *Journal of Marriage and the Family* 62(1): 54.

103 Waite and Gallagher. 2000; George A. Akerlof. 1998. "Men Without Children." *The Economic Journal* 108: 287–309; Steven L. Nock. 1998. "The Consequences of Premarital Fatherhood." *American Sociological Review* 63: 250–263; Joung. 1996.

104 Nock. 1998; Wilcox and Lerman. 2014.

105 Brandon G. Wagner. "Marriage, Cohabitation, and Sexual Exclusivity: Unpacking the Effect of Marriage." *Social Forces* 97(3): 1231–1256. https://doi.org/10.1093/sf/soy082.

106 Frisco, Wenger, and Kreager. 2016.

107 Nock. 1998.

108 Shelly Lundberg, Robert A. Pollak, and Jenna Stearns. 2016. "Family Inequality: Diverging Patterns in Marriage, Cohabitation, and Childbearing." *Journal of Economic Perspectives* 30(2): 79–102; Akerlof. 1998.

109 Lundberg, Pollak, and Stearns. 2016.

110 Nock. 1998.

111 Jennifer S. Mascaro, Patrick D. Hackett, and James K. Rilling. 2013. "Testicular Volume Is Inversely Correlated with Nurturing-related Brain Activity in Human Fathers." *Proceedings of the National Academy of Sciences* 110(39): 15746–15751. https://doi.org/10.1073/pnas.1305579110; Alan Booth and James M. Dabbs, Jr. 1993. "Testosterone and Men's Marriages." *Social Forces* 7 2(2): 463–77; T.C. Burnham, J. Flynn Chapman, Peter B. Gray, M. H. McIntyre, and Peter T. Ellison. "Men in Committed, Romantic Relationships Have Lower Testosterone." *Hormones and Behavior* 4 4(2): 119–22; Peter B. Gray *et al.* 2004. "Human Male Pair Bonding and Testosterone." *Human Nature* 15(2): 119–31; Peter B. Gray, Sonya M. Kahlenberg, Emily S. Barrett, Susan F. Lipson, and Peter T. Ellison. 2002. "Marriage and Fatherhood Are Associated with Lower Testosterone in Males." *Evolution and Human Behavior* 23(3): 193–201. Allan Mazur and Joel Michalek. 1998. "Marriage, Divorce, and Male Testosterone." *Social Forces* 77(1): 315–30; James Dabbs. 2000. *Heroes, Rogues, and Lovers: Testosterone and Behavior.* New York: McGraw-Hill.

112   Waite and Gallagher. 2000. P. 152.

113   Catherine T. Kenney and Sara S. McLanahan. 2006. "Why Are Cohabiting Relationships More Violent than Marriages?" *Demography* 43(1): 127–140; Wendy D. Manning, Monica A. Longmore, and Peggy C. Giordano. 2018. "Cohabitation and Intimate Partner Violence During Emerging Adulthood: High Constraints and Low Commitment." *Journal of Family Issues* 39(4): 1030–55. https://doi.org/10.1177/0192513X16686132.

114   Waite and Gallagher. 2000. P. 155.

115   Susan B. Sorenson and Devan Spear. 2018. "New Data on Intimate Partner Violence and Intimate Relationships: Implications for Gun Laws and Federal Data Collection." *Preventive Medicine* 107:103–108.

116   Waite and Gallagher. 2000. P. 155.

117   Wilcox and Nock. 2006.

118   *Ibid.*; Paul Amato and Stacy Rogers. 1999. "Do Attitudes toward Divorce Affect Marital Quality?" *Journal of Family Issues* 2 0: 69–86.

119   Scott M. Stanley, Sarah W. Whitton, and Howard J. Markman. 2004. "Maybe I Do: Interpersonal Commitment and Premarital or Nonmarital Cohabitation." *Journal of Family Issues* 2 5: 496–519; Wilcox *et al.* 2011.

120   To take just one example of this new modern effort to undermine the consensus, psychologist Bella DePaulo has published numerous works to dispel "myths" about marriage that she claims are based not on science but rather ideology alone. Her 2015 book, *Marriage vs. Single Life* is a collection of her endeavors to critique and dismantle many scientific studies with findings in favor of marriage. Yet her tactics provide excellent examples of the very things she decries. In a 2017 *New York Times* op-ed, DePaulo discussed a recent study by Matthijs Kalmijn from Switzerland, highlighting the component where people told researchers their estimates of their own health. Never-married individuals reported slightly better health ratings for themselves than did married people. Those who were divorced reported the worst health of the three groups. However, as Harvard epidemiologist Tyler VanderWeele points out, the study also found *positive* effects associated with entering marriage: less depression and increasing life satisfaction (and the reverse for becoming divorced). DePaulo side-stepped these findings in her op-ed. And while subjective health self-reports have some value, the ratings do not equate to actual health itself. The data we have already presented in this document include many objective measures of health, such as incidence of heart disease, odds of cancer recovery, states of mental health, and mortality rates. On average, VamderWeele finds that the married are at decreased risk of death in the next ten to twenty years, are more likely to be satisfied with life, and are less likely to become depressed than are the

unmarried. DePaulo, however, selectively reports on the findings that support what she calls the "newfound wisdom" that the link between marriage and health "just isn't so." On the basis of a single study's subjective health measure, she chooses to ignore the cumulative weight of decades of research. Predictably, this partisan presentation was broadly disseminated, and along with it a further obscuring of the value of marriage in the minds of the public. Bella DePaulo. 2015. *Marriage vs. Single Life: How Science and the Media Got It So Wrong.* CreateSpace Independent Publishing Platform. Bella DePaulo. 2017. "Get Married, Get Healthy? Maybe Not." *New York Times* May 25. https://www.nytimes.com/2017/05/25/opinion/marriage-health-study.html?_r=0. Matthijs Kalmijn. 2017. "The Ambiguous Link between Marriage and Health: A Dynamic Reanalysis of Loss and Gain Effects." *Social Forces* 95:1607–1636. Tyler VanderWeele. 2017. "What the *New York Times* Gets Wrong about Marriage, Health, and Well-being." *Institute for Family Studies Blog*, May 2017. https://ifstudies.org/blog/what-the-new-york-times-gets-wrong-about-marriage-health-and-well-being.

121   Adam Thomas and Isabel Sawhill. 2005. "For Love and Money? The Impact of Family Structure on Family Income." *The Future of Children* 15: 57–74. In addition, adolescents in middle- and upper-class homes were significantly more likely in 2017 to be living with their biological parents (77 percent versus 55 percent in working-class homes). See W. Bradford Wilcox and Wendy Wang. 2017. "The Marriage Divide: How and Why Working-class Families Are More Fragile Today." *Research Brief, September*. Charlottesville, VA: Institute for Family Studies. https://www.aei.org/publication/the-marriage-divide-how-and-why-working-class-families-are-more-fragile-today/.

122   Vanessa Sacks and David Murphey. 2018. "The Prevalence of Childhood Adverse Experiences, Nationally, by State, and by Race or Ethnicity." *Research Brief, June*. Washington, DC: Child Trends.

123   *Ibid.*

124   Amato. 2005. P. 89.

125   Danielle Kaeble and Mary Cowhig. 2018. "Correctional Populations in the United States, 2016." *Research Bulletin, April. NCJ 251211*. Washington, DC: Bureau of Justice Statistics, U.S. Department of Justice.

126   Urban Institute. 2017. "Police and Corrections Expenditures." *Research Bulletin*. Washington, DC: Urban Institute. https://www.urban.org/policy-centers/cross-center-initiatives/state-local-finance-initiative/state-and-local-backgrounders/police-and-corrections-expenditures.

127   Akerlof. 1998.

128   Robert J. Sampson. 1995. "Unemployment and Imbalanced Sex Ratios: Race
      Specific Consequences for Family Structure and Crime." In M.B. Tucker and C.
      Mitchell-Kernan, Eds. *The Decline in Marriage among African Americans*. New
      York: Russell Sage. P. 249.

129   Michael Rocque, Chad Posick, Steven E. Barkan, and Ray Paternoster.
      2014. "Marriage and County-Level Crime Rates: A Research
      Note." *Journal of Research in Crime and Delinquency* 52: 130–45. https://doi.
      org/10.1177/0022427814547113.

130   Isabel V. Sawhill. 1999. "Families at Risk." In H. Aaron and R. Reischauer,
      Eds. *Setting National Priorities: The 2000 Election and Beyond*. Washington, DC:
      Brookings Institution. For the connection of nonmarital births and divorce to
      federal and state welfare spending, see Robert Rector. 2001. "The Size and Scope
      of Means-tested Welfare Spending." *Research Brief, August*. Washington, DC: The
      Heritage Foundation. https://www.heritage.org/testimony/the-size-and-scope-
      means-tested-welfare-spending.

131   David Schramm. 2003. "Preliminary Estimates of the Economic Consequences of
      Divorce." Logan: Utah State University.

132   Benjamin Scafidi. 2008. *The Taxpayer Costs of Divorce and Unwed Childbearing:
      First-ever Estimates for the Nation and for All Fifty States*. New York: Institute for
      American Values.

133   Deborah M. Stone *et al.* 2018. "Vital Signs: Trends in the State Suicide Rates—
      United States, 1999–2016 and Circumstances Contributing to Suicide—27
      States, 2015." *Morbidity and Mortality Weekly Report* 67:617–624. http://dx.doi.
      org/10.15585/mmwr.mm6722a1.

134   Clay Routledge. 2018a. "Suicides Have Increased. Is This an Existential Crisis?"
      New York Times. June 23. https://www.nytimes.com/2018/06/23/opinion/sunday/
      suicide-rate-existential-crisis.html.

135   S. Katherine Nelson, Kostadin Kushlev, Tammy English, Elizabeth W. Dunn, and
      Sonja Lyubomirsky. 2013. "In Defense of Parenthood: Children Are Associated
      With More Joy Than Misery." *Psychological Science* 24(1): 3–10. https://doi.
      org/10.1177/0956797612447798. With respect to secularization, Routledge offers
      his own research to demonstrate that the meaningfulness found in religious faith is
      difficult to reproduce in other contexts. See Clay Routledge. 2018b. *Supernatural:
      Death, Meaning, and the Power of the Invisible World*. New York: Oxford University
      Press.

136   Anne Case and Angus Deaton. 2017. "Mortality and Morbidity in the
      21st Century." *Brookings Papers on Economic Activity* 2017: 397–476.

137 *Ibid.* P. 430.

138 *Ibid.* P. 431.

139 *Ibid.*

140 Bella DePaulo. 2018. "The Great Unraveling: Marriage Liberated Us by Becoming Undone." *Psychology Today.* October 1. https://www.psychologytoday.com/us/ blog/living-single/201810/the-great-unraveling-marriage-liberated-us-coming-undone.

141 Oren Cass *et al.* 2018. *Work, Skills, and Community: Restoring Opportunity for the Working Class.* Washington, DC: Opportunity America, The American Enterprise Institute for Public Policy Research, and The Brookings Institution.

142 Paul Amato and Alan Booth. 1997. *A Generation at Risk.* Cambridge: Harvard University Press.

143 Casey E. Copen, Kimberly Daniels, Jonathan Vespa, and William D. Mosher. 2012. "First Marriages in the United States: Data from the 2006–2010 National Survey of Family Growth." *National Health Statistics Reports* 49. Hyattsville, MD: National Center for Health Statistics.

144 Paul Hemez. 2017. "Divorce Rate in the U.S.: Geographic Variation, 2016." *Family Profiles* FP-17-24. Bowling Green, OH: National Center for Family and Marriage Research. https://www.bgsu.edu/ncfmr/resources/data/family-profiles/ hemez-divorce-rate-2016-fp-17-24.html.

145 Philip N. Cohen. 2018. "The Coming Divorce Decline." *SocArXiv* September 14. https://doi.org/10.31235/osf.io/h2sk6.

146 Ben Steverman. 2018. "Millennials Are Causing the U.S. Divorce Rate to Plummet." *Bloomberg* September 25. https://www.bloomberg.com/news/ articles/2018-09-25/millennials-are-causing-the-u-s-divorce-rate-to-plummet.

147 Wilcox and Wang. 2017.

148 Steverman. 2018.

149 Alan Booth and Paul R. Amato. 2001. "Parental Predivorce Relations and Offspring Postdivorce Well-being." *Journal of Marriage and Family* 63:197-212. https://doi. org/10.1111/j.1741-3737.2001.00197.x; Amato and Booth. 1997.

150 Booth and Amato. 2001; Leila Miller, Ed. 2017. *Primal Loss: The Now-Adult Children of Divorce Speak.* Phoenix, AZ: LCB; Judith S. Wallerstein, Julia M. Lewis, and Sandra Blakeslee. 2000. *The Unexpected Legacy of Divorce: The 25 Year Landmark Study.* New York: Hyperion.

151 Wilcox *et al.* 2011. Marquardt. 2005a. Wallerstein, Lewis, and Blakeslee. 2000.

152   Wilcox *et al.* 2011. McLanahan and Sandefur. 1994.

153   Vittorio Carlo Vezzetti. 2016. "New Approaches to Divorce with Children: A Problem of Public Health." *Health Psychology Open.* https://doi.org/10.1177/2055102916678105.

154   Wilcox *et al.* 2011. Martinuk. 2016.

155   Steven Stack and Jonathan Scourfield. 2015. "Recency of Divorce, Depression and Suicide Risk." *Journal of Family Issues* 36: 695–15. P. 696.

156   *Ibid.*

157   Martinuk. 2016.

158   Renee Stepler. 2017a. "Led by Baby Boomers, Divorce Rates Climb for America's 50+ Population." *Research Brief, March 5.* Washington, DC: Pew Research Center.

159   Teresa S. Collett. 2018. "Being Older Doesn't Make Divorce Any Wiser: Families Like Mine Fight to Buck Divorce Trend." *USA Today* September 6.

160   Norval Glenn. 1996. "Values, Attitudes, and the State of American Marriages." In D. Popenoe, J. Elshtain, and D. Blankenhorn, Eds. *Promises to Keep.* Lanham, MD: Rowman and Littlefield; Frank Furstenberg. 2001. "The Fading Dream: Prospects for Marriage in the Inner City." In E. Anderson and D. Massey, Eds. *Problem of the Century.* New York: Russell Sage.

161   Brienna Perelli-Harris, Ann Berrington, Nora Sánchez Gassen, Paulina Galezewska, and Jennifer A. Holland. 2017. "The Rise in Divorce and Cohabitation: Is There a Link?" *Population and Development Review* 43: 303–329.

162   Wilcox *et al.* 2011. P. 21.

163   Child Trends. 2018. "Births to Unmarried Women." *Research Brief, September.* Bethesda, MD: Child Trends.

164   Gretchen Livingston. 2018a. "About One-third of U.S. Children Are Living with an Unmarried Parent." *Research Brief, April 27.* Washington, DC: Pew Research Center.

165   Gretchen Livingston. 2018b. "The Changing Profile of Unmarried Parents." *Research Brief, April 25.* Washington, DC: Pew Research Center.

166   Lyman Stone. 2018. "Decades-long Rise in Nonmarital Childbearing Reverses." *Research Brief, August.* Charlottesville, VA: Institute for Family Studies.

167   Child Trends. 2018.

168   *Ibid.*

169   Kelly Musick and Katherine Michelmore. 2018. "Cross-National Comparisons of Union Stability in Cohabiting and Married Families with Children." *Demography* 55:1389–1421. https://doi.org/10.1007/s13524-018-0683-6.

170   R. Kelly Raley, Megan M. Sweeney, and Danielle Wondra. 2015. "The Growing Racial and Ethnic Divide in U.S. Marriage Patterns." *The Future of Children* 25(2): 89–109; Richard V. Reeves and Katherine Guyot. 2017. "Black Women Are Earning More College Degrees, but That Alone Won't Close Race Gap." *Research Brief, December.* Washington, DC: Brookings Institution.

171   U.S. Census Bureau. 2017. *2013–2017 American Community Survey 5-Year Estimates.* Washington, DC: U.S. Census Bureau.

172   Child Trends. 2018.

173   Guttmacher Institute. 2017. "Abortion Rates by Race and Ethnicity." *Fact Sheet, October*; Rachel K. Jones and Jenna Jerman. 2017. "Population Group Abortion Rates and Lifetime Incidence of Abortion: United States, 2008–2014." *American Journal of Public Health* 107(12): 1904–1909.

174   Susan A. Cohen. 2008. "Abortion and Women of Color: The Bigger Picture." *Guttmacher Policy Review* 11(3). https://www.guttmacher.org/gpr/2008/08/abortion-and-women-color-bigger-picture.

175   Guttmacher Institute. 2018. "Induced Abortion in the United States." *Fact Sheet, January.* https://www.guttmacher.org/fact-sheet/induced-abortion-united-states.

176   Jason L. Riley. 2018. "Let's Talk about the Black Abortion Rate." *Wall Street Journal* July 10. https://www.wsj.com/articles/lets-talk-about-the-black-abortion-rate-1531263697.

177   *Ibid.*

178   David Ribar. 2015. "Why Marriage Matters for Child Wellbeing." *The Future of Children* 25(2): 11–27; Wilcox *et al.* 2011.

179   Wilcox *et al.* 2011.

180   Daniel T. Lichter, Deborah Roempke Graefe, and J. Brian Brown. 2003. "Is Marriage a Panacea? Union Formation among Economically Disadvantaged Unwed Mothers." *Social Problems* 50: 60–86; Daniel T. Lichter, Christie D. Batson, and J. Brian Brown. 2004. "Welfare Reform and Marriage Promotion: The Marital Expectations and Desires of Single and Cohabiting Mothers." *Social Service Review* 38: 2–25; Lawrence L. Wu and Barbara Wolfe. 2001. *Out of Wedlock: Causes and Consequences of Nonmarital Fertility.* New York: Russell Sage.

181   Steven L. Nock. 1998. "The Consequences of Premarital Fatherhood." *American Sociological Review* 63: 250–263.

182   Wendy Wang and W. Bradford Wilcox. 2017. "The Millennial Success Sequence: Marriage, Kids, and the 'Success Sequence' among Young Adults." *Research Brief.* Washington, DC: American Enterprise Institute and Institute for Family Studies.

183   Sara McLanahan and Isabel Sawhill. 2015. "Marriage and Child Wellbeing Revisited: Introducing the Issue." *The Future of Children* 25(2): 3–9; Wendy D. Manning. 2015. "Cohabitation and Child Wellbeing." *The Future of Children* 25(2): 51–66; Sara McLanahan, Irwin Garfinkel, Ronald B. Mincy, and Elisabeth Donahue. 2010. "Introducing the Issue." *The Future of Children* 20(2): 3–16.

184   Popenoe and Whitehead. 2005.

185   Renee Stepler. 2017b. "Number of U.S. Adults Cohabiting with a Partner Continues to Rise, Especially among Those 50 and Older." *Research Brief, April 6.* Washington, DC: Pew Research Center.

186   In 2018, 9 percent of young adults (aged eighteen through twenty-four) were cohabiting, compared to 7 percent who lived with a spouse. Benjamin Gurrentz. 2018. "For Young Adults, Cohabitation Is Up, Marriage Is Down." *Research Brief, November.* Washington, DC: U.S. Census Bureau.

187   Martinuk. 2016.

188   Wilcox *et al.* 2011; Wilcox and Price. 2018.

189   Wilcox *et al.* 2011.

190   *Ibid.*

191   Michael J. Rosenfeld and Katharina Roesler. 2019. "Cohabitation Experience and Cohabitation's Association with Marital Dissolution." *Journal of Marriage and Family* 81(1): 42–58. https://doi.org/10.1111/jomf.12530; Scott Stanley and Galena Rhoades. 2018. "Premarital Cohabitation Is Still Associated with Greater Odds of Divorce." *Research Blog,* October 17. Charlottesville, VA: Institute for Family Studies.

192   Manning. 2015.

193   Livingston. 2018b. See also Laurie DeRose, Mark Lyons-Amos, W. Bradford Wilcox, and Gloria Huarcaya. 2017. "The Cohabitation-Go-Round: Cohabitation and Family Instability across the Globe." *Research Brief.* New York: Social Trends Institute.

194   Forty-nine percent of children born to college-educated mothers who are cohabiting at the time of their birth will experience parental separation before they turn twelve, compared to only 18 percent of those whose mothers are married when they are born. W. Bradford Wilcox and Laurie DeRose. 2017. "Ties That Bind." *Foreign Affairs* February 14.

195   Wilcox *et al.* 2011.

196   Manning. 2015.

197   Sedlak *et al.* 2010.

198   Patricia G. Schnitzer and Bernard G. Ewigman. 2005. "Child Deaths Resulting from Inflicted Injuries: Household Risk Factors and Perpetrator Characteristics." *Pediatrics* 116(5): e687–93. https://www.ncbi.nlm.nih.gov/pubmed/16263983.

199   Walter R. Schumm. 2018. *Same-sex Parenting Research: A Critical Assessment.* London: Wilberforce; Ana Samuel, Ed. 2014. *No Differences? How Children in Same-sex Households Fare: Studies from Social Science.* Princeton, NJ: Witherspoon Institute.

200   Benjamin G. Miller, Stephanie Kors, and Jenny Macfie. 2017. "No Differences? Meta-analytic Comparisons of Psychological Adjustment in Children of Gay Fathers and Heterosexual Parents." *Psychology of Sexual Orientation and Gender Diversity,* 4(1): 14–22.

201   Henny M. W. Bos, Justin R. Knox, Loes van Rijn-van Gelderen, and Nanette Gartrell. 2016. "Same-sex and Different-sex Parent Households and Child Health Outcomes: Findings from the National Survey of Children's Health." *Journal of Developmental & Behavioral Pediatrics* 37(3): 179–187.

202   Mark Regnerus. 2012. "How Different Are the Adult Children of Parents Who Have Same-sex Relationships? Findings from the New Family Structures Study." *Social Science Research* 41(4): 752–770.

203   Douglas W. Allen. 2013. "High School Graduation Rates among Children of Same-sex Households." *Review of Economics of the Household* 11: 635–658; Douglas W. Allen, Catherine Pakaluk, and Joseph Price. 2013. "Nontraditional Families and Childhood Progress through School: A Comment on Rosenfeld." *Demography* 50: 955–961; Douglas W. Allen, Catherine Pakaluk, and Joseph Price. 2014. "Normal Progress through School: Further Results." In A. Samuel, Ed. 2014. *No Differences? How Children in Same-Sex Households Fare.* Princeton, NJ. The Witherspoon Institute.

204   Caleb S. Watkins. 2018. "School Progress among Children of Same-sex Couples." *Demography* 55(3): 799–821. https://doi.org/10.1007/s13524-018-0678-3.

205   D. Paul Sullins. 2017a. "Harms Suffered by Children with Same-sex Parents—A Research Summary." https://truthandlove.com/wp-content/uploads/2017/06/Sullins-2-page-FINAL.pdf.

206   Regnerus 2012; Allen 2013; D. Paul Sullins. 2015a. "Emotional Problems among Children with Same-sex Parents: Difference by Definition." *British Journal of Education, Society and Behavioural Science* 7(2):99–120. http://dx.doi.org/10.2139/ ssrn.2500537. Note: While both Regnerus's and Sullins's studies have been widely attacked and criticized, the objections are more often ideological than scientific; none of their studies has been retracted. For a clear rebuttal, see Anderson. 2015. Note 30, P. 238–241. For a similar example, see D. Paul Sullins. 2016a. "Response to: Comment on 'Invisible Victims: Delayed Onset Depression among Adults with Same-sex Parents.' " *Depression Research and Treatment* 2016.

207   Michael Rosenfeld. 2010. "Nontraditional Families and Childhood Progress through School." *Demography* 47: 755–775. https://doi.org/10.1353/dem.0.0112; Jennifer L. Wainwright, Stephen T. Russell, and Charlotte J. Patterson. 2004. "Psychosocial Adjustment, School Outcomes, and Romantic Relationships of Adolescents with Same-sex Parents." *Child Development* 75(6): 1886–1898; Jennifer L. Wainright and Charlotte J. Patterson. 2006. "Delinquency, Victimization, and Substance Use among Adolescents with Female Same-sex Parents." *Journal of Family Psychology* 20(3): 526–30; Jennifer L.Wainright and Charlotte J. Patterson. 2008. "Peer Relations among Adolescents with Female Same-sex Parents." *Developmental Psychology* 44(1): 117–126.

208   D. Paul Sullins. 2015a. "The Unexpected Harm of Same-sex Marriage: A Critical Appraisal, Replication and Re-Analysis of Wainright and Patterson's Studies of Adolescents with Same-sex Parents." http://dx.doi.org/10.2139/ssrn.2589129; D. Paul Sullins. 2017a. Such errors continue to affect the research and necessitate corrections. For instance, see D. Paul Sullins. 2017b. "Sample Errors Call into Question Conclusions Regarding Same-sex Married Parents: A Comment on 'Family Structure and Child Health: Does the Sex Composition of the Parents Matter?'" *Demography* 54: 2375–2383. https://doi.org/10.1007/s13524-017-0616-9; Corinne Reczek, Russell Spike, Hui Liu, and Robert Crosnoe. 2017. "The Promise and Perils of Population Research on Same-sex Families." *Demography* 54(6): 2385–2397.

209   Sullins. 2015a. See also Schumm. 2018. In some cases, these findings disappear after controlling for household instability, raising questions both about elevated rates of family breakdown in same-sex households as well as appropriate ways to analyze associated data.

210   Sullins. 2015a.

211   Regnerus. 2012; Sullins. 2016b. "Invisible Victims: Delayed Onset Depression among Adults with Same-sex Parents." *Depression Research and Treatment* 2016. https://ssrn.com/abstract=2801825.

212   Sullins. 2016b.

213   Sullins. 2015a.

214   Reczek, Spike, Liu, and Crosnoe. 2017.

215   Sullins. 2015a.

216   Mark J. Stern. 2016. "The Scientific Debate about Same-sex Parenting Is Over." *Slate* April 13.

217   Bos, Knox, van Rijn-van Gelderen, and Gartrell. 2016. Far from proving the claim that the same-sex parenting debate is over, this study found that "female same-sex parents report more anger, irritation, and comparative frustration with their (apparently misbehaving) children than do opposite-sex parents." The authors of the study also failed to measure a full range of child outcomes. The authors did not include measures of "school progress, problems in school, participation in sports and recreational activities, volunteering, sleep, exercise, media consumption, reading, depression, bullying behavior, and all but one of five different measures of flourishing." Mark Regnerus. 2016. "Media Gush Over New Study, Only to Find Same-Sex Parents More Irritated with their Children." *Public Discourse* April 15. As Witherspoon Institute Senior Research Scholar Robert P. George has noted, "The valid, but difficult, way to justify a claim that 'the science is settled' is to establish by scientific methods the truth of the claim. The other way is to use power to stigmatize dissent, intimidate potential dissenters, and make questioning the claim dangerous to careers."

218   American Psychological Association. 2005. "Lesbian and Gay Parenting." *Research Brief*. Washington, DC: American Psychological Association; Loren Marks. 2012. "Same-sex Parenting and Children's Outcomes: A Closer Examination of the American Psychological Association's Brief on Lesbian and Gay Parenting." *Social Science Research* 41(4): 735–751; Mark Regnerus. 2016. "Hijacking Science: How the 'No Differences' Consensus about Same-sex Households and Children Works." *Public Discourse* October 14.

219   Regnerus. 2016.

220   Jessica N. Fish and Stephen T. Russell. 2018. "Queering Methodologies to Understand Queer Families." *Family Relations* 67: 12–25. P. 20; Linda Thompson. 1992. "Feminist Methodology for Family Studies." *Journal of Marriage and Family* 54: 3–18.

221   Abbie E. Goldberg. 2013. " 'Doing' and 'Undoing' Gender: The Meaning of Division of Housework in Same-sex Couples." *Journal of Family Therapy & Review* 5: 85–104. P. 33; Fish and Russell. 2018. P. 20.

222   Michael D. Kimmel. 2017. "Gay Marriage, Monogamy, and the Lure of Open Relationships." *Advocate* June 29; Mark Oppenheimer. 2011. "Married, with Infidelities." *New York Times* June 30.

223   Anderson. 2015. P. 161.

224   Sabrina Tavernise. 2018. "U.S. Fertility Rate Fell to a Record Low, for a Second Straight Year." *New York Times* May 16.

225   Fredrik DeBoer. 2015. "It's Time to Legalize Polygamy: Why Group Marriage Is the Next Horizon of Social Liberalism." *Politico* June 16; Anderson. 2015. P. 46.

226   Joseph Raz. 1986. *The Morality of Freedom.* Oxford: Clarendon Press. P. 162.

227   For examples, see Ryan T. Anderson. 2018. "Disagreement is Not Always Discrimination: On Masterpiece Cakeshop and the Analogy to Interracial Marriage." *Georgetown Journal of Law & Public Policy,* 16(1): 123–145. https://ssrn.com/abstract=3136750. See also Hindawi Limited. 2017. "Expression of Concern on 'Invisible Victims: Delayed Onset Depression Among Adults with Same-sex Parents.' " *Depression Research and Treatment* 2016; Sullins. 2016a.

228   U.S. Census Bureau. 2018. "Older People Projected to Outnumber Children for First Time in U.S. History." *CB18-41.* https://www.census.gov/newsroom/press-releases/2018/cb18-41-population-projections.html.

229   Anderson. 2018; Anderson. 2015.

230   Paul Peluso, Seth Eisenberg, and Rachel Schindler. 2011. "The Healthy Marriage and Responsible Fatherhood Impact Report Initiative: Relationship Education Impact Report." *Research Brief, September.* Pembroke Pines, FL: PAIRS Foundation. https://issuu.com/pairs/docs/impact_studies. See more at http://www.pairs.com.

231   For information on Retrouvaille, visit https://www.helpourmarriage.org.

232   Ron Haskins. 2015. "The Family Is Here to Stay—or Not." *The Future of Children,* 25(2):129–153. For a recent example of demonstrable success, see W. Bradford Wilcox and Spencer James. 2018. "Divorce Is Down in Duval County." *Research Brief.* Washington, DC: Philanthropy Roundtable.

233   Haskins. 2015; Cass *et al.* 2018.

234   Katherine Michelmore. 2018. "The Earned Income Tax Credit and Union Formation: The Impact of Expected Spouse Earnings." *Review of Economics of the Household* 16(2): 377–406. https://doi.org/10.1007/s11150-016-9348-7.

235   Haskins. 2015; Adam Carasso and C. Eugene Steuerle. 2005. "The Hefty Penalty on Marriage Facing Many Households with Children." *Future of Children* 15: 157–175.

236   Brian Tobin. 2018. "Donor-conceived Children: It's Time to Ban Anonymous Sperm Donation." *TheJournal.ie* June 26; Center for Bioethics and Culture. 2018. *I'm a Sperm Donor Father. Here's My Story.* Pleasant Hill, CA: The Center for Bioethics and Culture.

237   European Parliament. 2015. "On the Annual Report on Human Rights and Democracy in the World 2014 and the European Union's Policy on the Matter." November 30 Paragraph 114; The Economist. 2017. "As Demand for Surrogacy Soars, More Countries Are Trying to Ban It." *The Economist* May 13.

238   Center for Bioethics and Culture. 2018.

239   Anderson. 2015; Anderson. 2018.

240   Samuel Smith. 2018. "Christian Charity Agrees to Work with LGBT Couples to Resume Foster Care Work in Philly." *Christian Post* June 30.

241   Paul LeBlanc. 2018. "Masterpiece Cakeshop Wins Gay Wedding Supreme Court Case." *Newsweek* June 4; Anderson. 2018.

242   David French. 2018. "Colorado Defies the Supreme Court, Renews Persecution of a Christian Baker." *National Review* August 15. https://www.nationalreview.com/2018/08/colorado-civil-rights-commission-jack-phillips-case/

243   Andy Kroll. 2017. "Meet the Megadonor Behind the LGBTQ Rights Movement." *Rolling Stone* June 23.

244   Anderson. 2018.

245   Lisa Littman. 2018. "Rapid Onset Gender-Dysphoria in Adolescents and Young Adults: A Study of Parental Reports." *PLOS ONE* 13(8): e0202330. https://doi.org/10.1371/journal.pone.0202330.

246   Brown University. 2019. "Brown Statement on Gender Dysphoria Study." Press release. https://www.brown.edu/news/2019-03-19/gender.

247   *Ibid.*

248   Jeffrey S. Flier. 2018. "As a Former Dean of Harvard Medical School, I Question Brown's Failure to Defend Lisa Littman." *Quillette.* https://quillette.com/2018/08/31/as-a-former-dean-of-harvard-medical-school-i-question-browns-failure-to-defend-lisa-littman.

249   *Ibid.*

250   "Brown University and PLOS ONE: Defend Academic Freedom and Scientific Inquiry." 2018. Online petition. https://www.ipetitions.com/petition/brown-university-and-plos-one-defend-academic.

About the Witherspoon Institute

The Witherspoon Institute is an independent research center that works to enhance public understanding of the moral foundations of free and democratic societies.

Located in Princeton, New Jersey, the Institute promotes the application of fundamental principles of republican government and ordered liberty to contemporary problems through a variety of academic and other educational ventures.

The Witherspoon Institute carries out its educational mission by providing seminars and similar opportunities to high school, undergraduate, and graduate students to examine the moral foundations of political, philosophical, and social thought. Its online journal, *Public Discourse*, publishes daily articles to foster constructive public discussions about what the Institute believes to be the five pillars of every decent and dynamic society: the individual, the family, the university, the market economy, and the state. Finally, the Institute sponsors grass-roots efforts to educate the general public about the nature and importance of marriage and family life through its CanaVox initiative.

For more information about the work of the Witherspoon Institute, please visit www.winst.org.